Starve Better

Please visit us at

ApexBookCompany.com

Starve Better

Surviving the Endless Horror
of the Writing Life

Nick Mamatas

Apex Publications

Cover art by Andrew Rich
Cover and Book design by Aaron Leis

Apex Publications, LLC
www.apexbookcompany.com
PO Box 24323 Lexington, KY 40524

Contents

The Book of Lies

The Book of Life

Appendix

Introduction

I'VE BEEN WRITING AND EDITING PROFESSIONALLY FOR JUST over a decade now, and for most of that time I worked freelance. No health insurance. No steady paycheck. No spouse with a job of her own, or any savings. Ten years on a tightrope. There were some flush times, of course. Early on I managed to buy an inexpensive two-family home and played landlord. This was during the dot-com boom, so many business and arts magazines were ready to pay well for articles on the Next Big Thing, the latest IPO, and the New Economy that would never ever falter. I then experienced, first hand, the immediate faltering of everything. I spent an afternoon stabbing with a stick and collecting papers from the World Trade Center that had fluttered over the Hudson and into my little Jersey City backyard. Magazine after magazine collapsed, starting just days later, many citing the fact that their accounts receivable were buried under smoldering rubble in a quarantined part of town. (This excuse was largely nonsense, of course. Most of the magazines had been shedding pages since the economic crash of the previous spring.) The dot-coms had fallen from the tightrope, and nobody in publishing works with a net.

I've also been involved in the book trade—I've written or contributed to over fifty books, and have been the in-house editor of a dozen more, and all but one of them have come from the independent press. Soft Skull, Ben Bella, Prime, Night Shade, Disinformation, Cemetery Dance, Delirium, and now lovely Apex Publications, and more. Publishers come and go, too. One overprinted book, a single car accident, a misread ISBN printed in a major review, shenanigans with a distributor or a crank with a brother-in-law lawyer and fifty spare bucks with which to file a nuisance lawsuit—this is how independent publishers can falter too. The only thing I can guarantee for readers of *Starve Better* is this: your checks will not arrive on time. You'll open your first book and alight upon an infelicity or copy error that will make you cringe. Friends and relatives will report that for the life of them they cannot find your book in stores anywhere, but they'll have good advice: send your book to Brad Pitt, and he might make a movie out of it!

If I had to do the last decade over, I probably wouldn't, and not because things have gone poorly for me. My nonfiction has been cited in academic journals, reprinted in daily newspapers, landed me on NPR (where I was called a "whore" for thirty minutes by the interviewer), and on one glorious day in 2006, generated $6,000 for me in a single very long stretch at the keyboard. My fiction has thrice been nominated for Bram Stoker awards, has been or will soon be published in Italian, German, and Greek, and has appeared everywhere from slick men's magazines to photocopied fanzines. As an editor, I've been nominated for the Hugo and World Fantasy awards. I now have a full-time job, my first ever with withholding and health insurance and a 401K, running my own science fiction and fantasy imprint. (Fewer than one job of this type opens up each year.) I wouldn't do it over because really, it's a dreadful life, freelancing as a writer—and as an almost willfully anti-commercial writer at that, with no academic pedigree or the cultural capital with which to gain a full-time appointment at a university. You can be commercial and do well, or be a full-time instructor and write what you like during the summer, but if you're not one or the other, you'll suffer as I have suffered.

Despite my many failures, I've done that which you're not supposed to do—published novellas without being "a name" (I am still not a name), published first-person essays in magazines that never run them, had my fiction featured in a German music magazine's 25th anniversary issue as the first and last short story ever to grace those pages, had people stop me in the street to ask if I were me ("Who's askin'?" is the best answer, I've found). I type with two fingers. I make fun of the publishing industry and its foibles on my blog. Pretty much the only sane thing I've done recently is name this book *Starve Better*—its original title was *The Nickronomicon*, which surely would have limited the potential audience of this book to the two dozen people who both keep track of my career and have the disposable income to buy a pamphlet. They're mostly blog readers. Maybe I'll save the original title for an omnibus collection of my Lovecraftian work . . . .

Indeed, *Starve Better* came about thanks largely to my blog. After writing some little piece of advice, I'd often get a comment or two along the lines of "You should collect all these little essays into a book." Finally, I asked myself "Why not?" And here you have it. I've not actually written enough appropriate blog posts to make a book, but I've also taught writing and have lecture notes, published a few essays on the writing life, and had the time to put down a few more thoughts here and there.

The first section is The Book of Lies, which consists of some notes on writing fiction, specifically short fiction. The second is The Book of Life, which details some advice on being a freelance writer of nonfiction, primarily of articles for magazines and alternative newspapers. We're concentrating on short subjects mainly because we're in the market for fast money, not good money. Writing a fantasy trilogy or a 10,000 word think piece on Henry Kissinger is all well and good, except that by the time the late check arrives for that sort of work, you've *been* off the tightrope and the birds have had their fill of your dead flesh. I cannot teach you how to avoid the traps of being a starving writer, but in this volume I hope I can teach you how to starve better.

Nick Mamatas
—Berkeley, California
July 2010

Starve Better

For Kazzie, who can't read any of this,
but who was there near the beginning.

[But first, a word of warning. Two, actually. The first is that I am a fan of pro wrestling. Sorry. The second is that all advice is contingent and partial. If you read something here, or anywhere else, that you don't want to do, then don't do it. Find another way to achieve your goals—either aesthetic or financial—as a writer. There is always another way. You may have to develop it yourself, but there is always another way. This essay comes from Flytrap, *a fun fanzine published by the award-winning author Tim Pratt and his wife, Heather Shaw, a wonderful writer in her own right.]*

All Advice is Terrible Advice, Plus Other Useful Advice

ADVICE ABOUT WRITING REMINDS ME OF NOTHING SO MUCH as the underrated feud between The Undertaker and the late Yokozuna in the early 90s WWF. The Undertaker was and is a stiff and Yokozuna was a butterball better suited for a sideshow than athletic exhibitions, but there was an element of unpredictability that gave their matches something special. I remember watching their infamous Casket Match at 1994's Royal Rumble with my then-roommate who took great joy in reminding me that wrestling was "fake." Yes, yes it is. Also fake: situation comedies, Farscape, soap operas, and half the news. This is known. Doesn't make the television less entertaining.

But my roommate just loved pointing out how fake it all was. During the match, the goal of which is to shove one's opponent into a coffin and shut him in, Pablo pointed out that the match was no-disqualification—the only rule was that the match ended when the casket was closed. "If it's no rules," demanded Pablo, "why don't ten bad guys show up, beat the shit out of the Undertaker, and shove him into the casket?"

About a minute later, that's exactly what happened. He shut up after that.

Those ten guys remind me of writing. There are no rules. Only the results matter; the process of shoving the kind-hearted zombie mortician into the rented coffin is irrelevant. The problem is that when people can't get results they want, they become obsessed with process. Nobody holds forth on the writing advice like barely published neophyte writers, and it makes me want to get together a posse of masked men and beat them down.

Recently, I got to witness somebody flip out over adverbs. The Harry Potter books, you see, are full of 'em. If you're flying, it's swiftly, if you're tip-toeing, it's stealthily. This, according to Mister Flippy, was wrong. "When editors see -ly words from newbies, the submission goes right into the round file! Why can Rowling get away with it?" he wanted to know. He had a readymade answer, too—money-grubbing publishers foolishly allowed adverbs into Harry Potter titles because the books sell. Big Name Authors can break the rules.

Of course they can. So can you. Using lots of adverbs and adjectives is a newbie mistake. Declaring the use of adverbs and adjectives forbidden due to some secret publishing industry decree is another newbie mistake. Engaging in conspiracy theory about the adverbs you do happen to see in books is a medical mistake by the newbie's doctor. Up the dosage, Bones.

There are a lots of little nonsensical shorthand rules. Don't write in first person. Really really don't write in second person. Make sure you spend equal time and effort on plot, characterization, themes, and facts. Be stylish. Don't be too stylish. Write to entertain only, don't be a pretentious Little Miss Fancy Britches. Make your prose purple and poetic so it stands out as something other than hackwork. Don't write a series of short stories and expect to sell them as a book. These rules are all about as useful for writing as they are for casket matches. Stories and books breaking all of these rules can be found on the shelves of every bookstore and library in America. That means that they aren't really rules. Look around, you'll see.

What are you going to believe, some nutcase on an online forum, or the evidence of your senses?

Even worse than the advice about what to write is the advice about how to write. Just a week ago I was in some chat room when a neophyte writer declared that writing short stories teaches one "the form" of writing novels. That sounded odd to me since short stories are a different form entirely. Plus, evidence of the senses: there are plenty of great novelists who write lousy short stories, and many excellent short story writers whose novels collapse utterly. Some masters of one form can literally not write the other form at all.

So I asked for evidence. The neophyte, a Clarion grad, pointed to Clarion. Plenty of Clarion grads have gone on to write novels. Many have not. Plenty of the Clarion alum novels blow rubber donkey dongs. Many are wonderful. Same as non-Clarion grads, really. I mentioned this. She put me on /ignore, as she was tired of hearing my non-existent "jabs." I found her website and checked out her bibliography. She hasn't mastered the novel yet, let's just say. Or gotten beyond the "fluke sale" short story level. All rules, no results. It's a common malady. After all, reading books on writing feels like writing, as does workshopping stories, handing in "crits," and holding forth in chat rooms. But those are all just preliminaries: literary pyrotechnics and entrance music, the catchphrases and snarled threats from someone who hasn't gotten sweaty yet. The only thing that matters is what goes on in the ring, and that ring is the editor's desk.

Even writers who do get results seem trapped in a rule mentality. I was reading a good short story writer's blog the other day; he had an interesting essay about the time he spent writing his first novel. The thrust of the entry was that he felt bad for taking so many days off while writing. My reaction was a simple "buh?" The novel is done. The novel seems very likely to sell. What do these days off matter? There's no guarantee that finishing the novel sooner would have made it sell more quickly, or that the book's quality suffered for the days he took off. It was just a neo-Calvinist self-administered spanking. "I" whack! "must" smack! "write" wham! "every" pow! "day!" crack! Talk like that makes Yokozuna cry. Winning's the name of the game here, not anything else. If the novel sells and is well-received, taking days off is, by definition, a successful strategy for writing a novel.

The cult of advice is insidious, even though many good writers know to preface their commentary with plenty of disclaimers and qualifiers. Unfortunately, when someone pays for a workshop or an MFA or a book on writing, they want to get what they pay for: The Secret to Writing Well. And if they don't get it, they'll just pretend that they do. Carefully qualified suggestions become God's own commandments.

One more story, this one neophyte versus neophyte: it seems that a pal of mine heard from Samuel R. Delany that plots are an artifact of the reading experience rather than intrinsic to the writing process, and that writers should understand this. She shared this pearl with some online buddies, who hooted and laughed and declared that Delany must be nuts. Their cries of "You have to have a plot!" were met with the equally tedious counterclaim "No, you can't have a plot, because there is no such thing!" Now, Delany has shoved quite a few grapplers into caskets in his day, so his comments are worth taking seriously. They are not worth taking as true, though, since clearly people have conceived of plots or something-they-call-plots and have created good, saleable stories that way, too.

Write what you want, when you want, and how you want to write it. If you keep finding yourself staring up at the lights while the ref counts to three, try another strategy. There are plenty to choose from. One thousand different writers work in one thousand different ways. Whether it's with the help of ten masked workshoppers, a set of brass knuckles hidden in one's stylish sequined trunks, or with the textbook execution of a hip-toss drive, whatever gets the story published and enjoyed is what works.

The Book of Lies

[My primary interest in fiction is the short story. I enjoy both commercial fiction—mostly science fiction, fantasy, and horror—and also transgressive, postmodern, experimental fiction. Thanks to these influences, my own works ends up being the most uncommercial sort of commercial fiction. This is why I have zero money. It is also why I've managed to publish SF in men's magazines with a quarter of a million readers for four-digit checks and in hotsy-totsy literary journals run by foreign governments and read almost exclusively by tenure committees . . . . And, I've been able to parlay my fiction into some nonfiction. This piece first appeared in the June 2009 issue of The Writer, *which is the best of the hobbyist magazines on writing, mainly because it does not let the ads—increasingly for self-publication services—dictate editorial policy, unlike some of its competitors. Of course, they did re-title the piece "In Praise of the Short Story" because hobby magazines have to be "up" at all times.]*

Why Write What Nobody Reads?
A Defense of the Short Story

HERE'S A WAY TO PASS THE TIME. QUIZ YOUR FRIENDS—THE ones who aren't themselves writers or aspiring writers—with a single question: "Read any good short stories lately?" The answer will likely be "No," except for the occasional reader of The New Yorker or perhaps a fan of science fiction or mystery who still reads the remaining magazines in those genres. Most literary journals have circulations in the lower four digits and more submitters than subscribers. Nor do most of them pay in anything but contributor copies, and if you happen to place your story with an online magazine, you'll get as many copies as you like as long as the printer toner holds out. Long gone are the days when The Saturday Evening Post was on six million coffee tables and its table of contents promised stories by everyone from William Faulkner to Ray Bradbury. That era will never return. So, then, why write short stories? There are several reasons that keep me toiling away in the comma mines, and perhaps they'll inspire you as well.

Freedom! Sweet, sweet freedom! The very anti-commercial status of short stories is a large part of what makes writing them worthwhile. The past few decades have seen a tightening in the New York—and even within the small and university—presses when it comes to book-length fiction. A work that falls "between genres" or that is shorter than 60,000 words (or longer than 150,000) isn't going to get much traction with agents and editors. Any novel that is structurally unusual or doesn't have Hollywood-ready protagonists is a hard sell, both to the publishing industry and to the public. Authors increasingly need a "platform" as a blogger, a past as a trauma survivor, or a telegenic cutie-pie face to get attention for their novels.

Individual short stories can be utterly wild and experimental, and their authors don't need to become the literary equivalent of used car salespeople to publish them. A single short story won't ruin sales for an issue of a magazine or journal, so editors can err on the side of quality rather than safety. Literary journals cover a wide aesthetic spectrum: from contemporary realism to obscure experimentation, from microfiction to novelettes. Even the commercial magazines take chances—the days of pulp hacks writing strictly to formula are long gone. In a recent issue of *Woman's World*, for example, author Christine

Pedersen published a romance story told from the point of view of a 1956 Ford Thunderbird. You just can't do that in romance novels.

With short fiction, you get to write (and publish) what you want. If edits need to be made, they'll be made by an editor and not by a corporate accountant, salesperson, or publicist.

Quick Money! This reason to write short fiction may seem a bit counter-intuitive. Many literary journals pay in nothing but contributor copies and prestige. The commercial fiction magazines pay around a nickel a word, whereas for short nonfiction, payments of twenty-five cents to a dollar a word aren't unreasonable. And then there's the competition. It's not unusual for a new writer to collect hundreds of rejections and to finally give up on a dozen or more stories before finally getting published. But there is money to be made in short fiction, and compared to writing novels, the money can come quickly. We're talking fast money, not good money.

In commercial fiction, especially science fiction and fantasy, there are a fairly large number of magazines and anthologies that pay anywhere from five to ten cents a word for short stories and novellas. A 5,000-word story written over a weekend can earn its author $250. To the right market, a 1,000-word story can be sold for $1,000. (And that's Woman's World, not Esquire.) Horror, mystery/crime, and even romance have a number of paying markets for short work as well, and acceptances (or rejections) come after weeks or months. That novel advance payment can be a year away, and that's even after signing the contract. Short fiction checks can come in time for Christmas . . . if you spend Labor Day weekend writing.

While literary journals don't *always* pay for short fiction, plenty do. Not only do the commercial slicks

(*The New Yorker*, *Playboy*) pay extremely well, there are venerable journals such as *Paris Review* and *Glimmer Train Stories* that pay hundreds of dollars. Less remunerative, but still worth paying attention to when it comes to earning money with short fiction, are avant-garde journals such as *Black Warrior Review*, the Canadian *subTERRAIN* and many others. Of course, many journals also run contests that involve paying a fee for the chance at a larger "prize," but there are enough paying literary journals and magazines to submit to before breaking out one's own checkbook for anything other than stamps and paper.

Is it even worthwhile to try to sell short stories for such small sums when one can just publish short fiction on a personal website or non-paying market? Well, take a look at your phone bill, cable bill, or that restaurant you like, or that new pair of shoes you want—a short story check can come in handy. It's a truism that nobody can make a living writing short stories anymore, but it's also true that nobody wants to spend forty or fifty hours a week cranking the little devils out. Think of short fiction as a sideline, or as a hobby that can turn a profit.

There is room for new authors for those publishing slots in the commercial and little magazines. Many writers cut their teeth on short fiction but soon move on to publishing novels. For them, the choice of spending a few days writing a short story for $500 or using that time to write a chapter of a book that can earn a $50,000 advance is clear—the novel takes precedence. Some prominent authors still write and publish short fiction despite the algebra of profit-per-keystroke, but many leave short fiction behind. Those authors who do continue writing short fiction even after becoming established as a novelist are most likely familiar with the ultimate reason to write short fiction.

Candy is Dandy and Liquor is Quicker, But Writing is Exciting! In the film *Art School Confidential,* a drunken cynic gives away the game to a young upstart by telling him the truth about a life in the arts:

> "What do you think an artist cares about? Does he think all day about fine wines and black tie affairs and what he's gonna say at the next after-dinner speech? No, he lives only for that narcotic moment of creative bliss."

Writing short fiction is a natural high. There is something about the short story, perhaps related to Edgar Allan Poe's notion of "the unity of effect or impression" that makes writing short stories, or at least finishing short stories, exhilarating. Unlike a novel, a short story's plot or throughline can be kept in one's own head as a single compelling thought or image. Making that thought manifest on the page is a euphoric thrill. Finishing a novel is a gas as well, but it can take months or years to get to the high. With short stories, you can experience "that narcotic moment of creative bliss" more frequently, and unlike the other rewards of writing—acceptance letters, checks, one's name in print—the glory of creation never gets old. Indeed, as one gets better at writing and thus better able to achieve the unity of effect, the emotion that comes from completing a short story grows even more intense. It's so for me, anyway, and given the huge numbers of people who continue to write short fiction when they could be writing work with a larger audience and larger checks attached, it must be a pretty common experience. This is the ultimate defense of the short story: is there any way to have more fun in front of a computer, alone, wearing all your clothes, and actually producing something rather than simply consuming? Not to me.

Aside:
. . . Or Not! Why You Shouldn't Write Short Stories

There are excellent reasons to write short stories, but also many poor ones. Many an aspiring writer ends up frustrated due to bad advice. Here are some common reasons why people write short stories . . . and why to ignore them.

It's "Easier" Than Writing a Novel. Short stories are, by definition, shorter than writing a novel, so clearly they'd be easier, right? Not necessarily. Many writers think at novel length, and their attempts at short fiction end after 10,000 words with their protagonists just getting out of bed. And if you're not already an enthusiastic reader of short stories, writing them isn't going to be easy at all.

It's "Practice" For Writing a Novel. Not any more than the hundred-meter dash is practice for running a marathon. Despite the centuries of innovation and evolution, Poe is still right—plot, character, pacing, and everything else is subordinate to unity of effect in short fiction, which can be read in a single sitting. A novel is just a different beast, and outside of the basics of sentence structure, short stories are not always the best training ground for would-be novelists.

You "Must" Write Stories Before Writing a Novel. It's true that short stories can get a new writer some attention, and that such attention can make publishing a novel easier. However, plenty of novelists debut without ever having published any short fiction, and many writers publish a handful of mediocre stories and then never go on to publish a novel, or publish their first books without their short fiction bibliography being a factor. If you're writing short stories only to be seen as "a real writer" so that you can then become a novelist, you're better off just revising your novel.

You Can Be Famous! Raymond Carver never published a novel. But even he wanted to be a novelist. You're no Raymond Carver.

[This is a new piece, but the metaphors are old ones, from "Depth of Field" in the book On Writing Horror, Mort Castle, *ed. It's a book well worth reading, and it's also one of the few titles I've been a part of that actually pays out royalty checks. Sure, it's $5 every June and December, but every royalty check is a gift. Mostly, one never sees a check in an anthology, as royalties are often split 50/50 between the editor and the mass of contributors. So if you sell short subjects to anthologies, don't spend a lot of time hanging around the mailbox.]*

All Pistons Firing

WHEN WRITING SHORT STORIES, MANY WRITERS GROW concerned with getting the story right. Short stories, they figure, need good characters, strong plots, interesting sentences, compelling themes, and exquisite pacing. When a story has all of the above, and all pistons are firing, surely publication will be a cinch. But no. The "all pistons firing" conception of the short story, though taught frequently in writing courses and detailed in how-to manuals of all sorts, is rather wrongheaded. Stories with good plots, good characters, good sentences, good themes, and good pacing aren't good stories. They're mediocre stories.

Of course, such stories are mediocre partially because of the production process—a writer hoping to get everything right may often think to herself, "Ah, in this paragraph I'll put in some character stuff. Then to move on the plot a bit. And to keep folks reading, I'll do something really cool with this sentence at the beginning of this paragraph." The paragraphs end up disconnected, the story awkwardly lurching from moment to moment for little reason. (Pacing often suffers the most, but the bad writer tries to make up for it by using single-sentence paragraphs.) All pistons are firing, but not in cooperation with one another.

Further, an all-pistons-firing author ultimately has little to say. Perhaps she wishes to make a great point about a character, or show off her clever sentences, or to put on a great show of a twisty and meaty plot . . . but she nevertheless expends just as much energy on the parts of the story that are less interesting. Even worse, she may spend more narrative space than is needed—in a short story we don't always have the room to learn all about the background and personality of characters while also experiencing an exciting plot. A great theme can be obscured by wonderful sentences. Almost by definition, to write an interesting story one must make choices regarding emphasis.

The all-pistons-firing metaphor is often itself to blame for misleading writers. Indeed, even editors are often confused by the hegemonic piston metaphor and find themselves unable to give their submitters any guidance other than, "We just want good stories." Short stories should be reconceptualized. Forget pistons, think photos.

Photographs, like short stories (which are generally read in a single sitting) represent a completed action. One can and should look at photographs carefully and intently, but they can be apprehended in a moment. And what makes a good photo but selective composition and focus? What makes a mediocre photo? Trying to get everything in frame and giving every element being photographed equal importance. A story isn't like a smoothly running engine, but is rather like a photograph. Photos can never be a perfect representation of what an eye looking at the same subject will see, partially due to the limitations of lenses and emulsions, but largely due to the conscious choice of the photographer. Photographers manipulate the focus of their work to highlight certain elements and occult others. Depth of field is a subjective quality; a photo that shows the petal of a single flower in perfect focus while fuzzing out the other petals or the stem and the leaves around the flower is as beautiful and worthy as a photo of an entire garden, where every flower is a sharp but minor part of the landscape.

When writing a story, choose a focus. Ultimately, you'll discover your strengths and weaknesses. This collection of strengths and weaknesses are what we call, in the writing game, *style*. As with all things, when writing a short story, you should concentrate on your strengths and work to minimize the importance of your weaknesses as they relate to that particular piece of fiction.

Kelly Link is not known for her plots; Raymond Carver is not known for his themes. Both of these writers concentrate on their strengths, as does any successful short story writer. Those writers whose work appears most often in *Analog*, the hard science fiction magazine, are strong when it comes to dramatizing scientific principles. Few members of the "Analog Mafia" will ever sell a short story to *Glimmer Train* or *Paris Review*. The literary authors who appear in those journals would almost certainly mess up the science if they tried to write hard SF. But each set of writers focuses on their strengths the way a photographer focuses on a certain element of a scene, and those strengths lead to publication, an audience, and a check.

Focus is vital. One of the greatest short stories of all time, "Araby" by James Joyce, is virtually without action. For lovers of thrilling plots, the story of a bashful boy attending a fair after promising to bring a girl a present, but then being too shy and too disappointed in the Araby (and in life itself, and himself) to do so, is inaccessible. But if our narrator was shooting elephants or foiling the plots of Communist scientists, Joyce never would have reached his thematic goals. Closer to home in the horror genre, had Thomas Ligotti actually introduced a real character *or* plot into his stellar story "The Red Tower," it would have fallen apart utterly. Both authors knew to choose a single focus and concentrate on it.

The photography metaphor supersedes the piston metaphor, but there is something to be learned from considering plot, character, theme, writing, and pacing individually. In order to concentrate on one's strengths, one has to have some strengths in the first place. Exploring the different elements of story can be handy in that regard. But, in the end, you have to transcend piston-firing. That's why instead of the remainder of this section dealing with the various "pistons," we will take a look at structural elements that most newer writers tend to stumble over. When you master the structure of the short story, you can better develop your strengths.

[When I was editing Clarkesworld Magazine, *I was often able to reject twenty stories in a single day, simply by reading only the first few paragraphs of each story. Beginnings are especially important when it comes to short stories—partially because every word counts and partially because there are hundreds of stories for an editor to read. Too bad the advice given to aspiring short story writers is so bad . . . .]*

Don't Throw the Hook

THE CULT OF ADVICE HAS MISLED MANY A SHORT STORY writer. Here's an insidious piece of advice you've surely heard before: Your short story has to start strong, with a hook.

On one level, it isn't even bad advice. Often, writers do just sit down and start writing. They have no idea how to begin a story, so they often begin at the beginning—with their protagonist waking up. Or perhaps with a lengthy bit of scene-setting, or the weather, or a snippet from a historical artifact or newspaper article. Pages and pages of background information, or the results of research, or tooling around with breakfast foods, keep the reader from getting to the story for pages and pages. The most common variations are especially deadly—I once had a streak of five stories in a row that featured a protagonist awaking confused in a strange room. Even if the fifth story was actually very good and absolutely required such an opening, I was already poisoned by its competitors. (Don't fret, though; I walked my dog and came back to the fifth story after a short break. It was *terrible*.)

One gets the feeling that even the author isn't sure about his or her story, so just writes until something

25

interesting comes to mind. This is perfectly fine, so long as one recognizes where the interesting story *starts*, and slices off the uninteresting part. Further, there is nothing intrinsically wrong with a story that takes a little while to rev up. In the nineteenth century, this sort of thing was not uncommon. "The Repairer of Reputations" by Robert W. Chambers (1895) spends seven hundred words on the state of the country before we are finally introduced to a character. It works, because the first-person narrator is a bit loopy, and rather obsessed with his position in the imperial dynasty of America. It also works because the introductory material is actually interesting.

The flaw of the "Gotta have a hook!" advice is that it leads to a secondary error on the part of many writers. Having heard that new writers tend to have a few pages of nonsense up front and that stories have to be engaging from the get-go, they often create an energetic first paragraph full of gun fights, monsters, characters cursing ("Fuuuuck!" or "Oh SHIT!" are very common story openings these days), and various other "hooks." Then, almost invariably, the author reveals that the gunfights are on TV, the monsters from a dream, the cursing character has woken up with a back spasm or is simply stuck in traffic (indeed, "stuck in traffic" might be the new "just woken up") and *then* we have the several pages of nonsense before the story actually begins. Rather than correcting the error of a boring beginning by eliminating the boring beginning or by changing the story's structure so that it is interesting from beginning to end, they simply added some "action" up top.

At first, I was fooled and would actually keep reading perhaps as much as a page before sending out a rejection letter, but soon enough it was easy for me to tell which beginnings were part of an organic whole and which were clumsy narrative prefixes to a mediocre story. Editors know.

The issue of the beginning "hook" is also important when it comes to first-person narrators, especially those who tell their stories in the past tense. The question that must be asked by the author as he or she writes such a story is this: *What story is my first-person narrator telling, and why?* "The Repairer of Reputations" answers these questions like so: "He is telling the story of what he believes will be his triumph and conquest of the United States" and "Because he's a crazy person." The extended history detailed in the opening is thus a way of building both character and setting (a futuristic New York of the 1920s, complete with public suicide booths).

Sadly, many people don't know why their characters are telling their stories, and thus have no idea how their characters should explain the events they've lived through or observed. These stories are often crippled by their openings: the character either starts at the beginning ("I woke up on a Tuesday . . . ") or with some compelling opening ("There was a knife to my throat!") followed by an extended piece of narrative backfill ("It had all started on Tuesday morning, when I woke up . . .).

The best way to handle first-person narrators speaking in the past tense is to remember that they want to tell the reader about the important part of the story, and they have to keep the reader interested in the same way you have to keep a listener interested when telling an anecdote about your daily life to someone. For example, imagine if, on your trip to a grocery store, you encountered a dragon. What would you tell your friends?

> Guess what I saw at the grocery store? A dragon!
> It was huge and right there in the frozen food aisle.
> I was so curious I followed it around the store

and then . . . [the rest of the story, including—one hopes—some interaction with the dragon that you found enlightening or interesting].

Or:

I got up yesterday and realized that I was out of milk. I like to have milk in my coffee every morning, so I decided to go to the store. I ran to get my shoes on and didn't even check my email first because if I dawdled I'd be late to work. Walking down the block, I composed a shopping list in my head. I needed milk, of course, but what about dinner? I decided I'd get some chicken, but also a few TV dinners because I'd heard it was going to snow over the weekend, and I needed some toilet paper as well, and I also wanted to get some high-fiber cereal. And so I got my cart and entered the store and trotted over to the dairy section and got my milk and then I swung over to frozen foods and there I saw a dragon.

Personally, I would have stopped listening to my dragon-spotting friend at "dawdled." If the dragon is the hook, it is buried too deeply and there is nothing compelling us to dig for it through the mass of quotidian detail. If the *milk* is the hook, well . . . .

"Start with a hook" is bad advice, ultimately, because of the word "hook." A hook is an important part of a story to be sure, and could do anywhere. It is the motor of the story—it can be the twist at the end, the broad concept, the compelling change a character undergoes, the language or clever structure of a piece . . . whatever makes a story worth reading is its hook. A hook may go in the beginning, but it need not. Beginnings are for something else. The start of a story, its first paragraph, should assure the reader that they are in capable hands. The beginning of the story should tantalize, not hook, the reader.

[When teaching at Grub Street Inc., Boston's premiere writer's center, I'd spend an hour talking about the pair of sentences that are the topic of this chapter. Despite the fact that stories are made out of sentences, genre fiction writers often pooh-pooh a focus on them. "Writing shouldn't get in the way of the story," we're told by successful writers, by busy editors, and by more than a few well-trained readers. Yet the best genre fiction contains sentences that can stand with Faulkner, Joyce, or anyone else an angry English professor might care to name. Write well; it makes things easier.

Definitely read Farewell, My Lovely the moment you have the chance.]

The Sentence

COMMERCIAL FICTION DOES NOT VALORIZE THE SENTENCE on the same level that literary fiction does. Indeed, many literary sorts and genre types agree—the genre isn't where to go to read good sentences. For the literary fiction reader and writer, the relative lack of excellent sentences is proof positive that genre writing is inferior. For the genre reader and writer, this same quality is often a point of pride. Writers brag that their sentences don't "get in the way" of the story—a bizarre sentiment since stories are made out of sentences—and Isaac Asimov's old saw about the "stained glass" of prose as contrasted with his preference: plate glass, which "is the equivalent of writing that is plain and unadorned. Ideally, in reading such writing, you are not even aware that you are reading. Ideas and events seem merely to flow from the mind of the writer into that of the reader without any barrier between."

It is certainly so that genre writing can benefit from plain sentences. The legendary Edward D. Hoch published hundreds of short mystery stories and had a story appear in every issue of *Ellery Queen's Mystery Magazine* for thirty-five years. His sentences had all the finesse of a cow's moo mid-tip, but his Nick Velvet series and other stories worked very well. The problem for the writer looking to make quick money writing shorts is that the plain style is so ubiquitous that the comparative advantage in writing like Asimov or Hoch is non-existent at this point. A good way to stand out from the immense competition is to pay more attention to sentences.

Despite the claims of both literary and genre writers, and the evidence of bad stories, some of the best sentences ever written can be found in genre fiction. Here are two, which work best in combination:

> It was a blonde. A blonde to make a bishop kick
> a hole in a stained-glass window.

We don't talk about the context of these sentences very much, as we can actually build some context just from these few words. That's what makes these sentences as efficiently written as any, but also much more than that. They are "plain and unadorned," as Asimov would recommend, but the ideas and events being transmitted are very different from the usual sort of description of an attractive woman one might read in a genre story.

The first sentence ain't much. The second is a doozy, but much of its juice comes from the first. Raymond Chandler knows how to write a sentence and he knows how to place it. Occasionally, one hears a sneer that genre writing is "workmanlike" or perhaps even "efficient," and this is so, but efficiency is a form of beauty, too. There are certainly plenty of bad sentences in genre fiction—"It was a blonde" in isolation certainly counts. ("It?" An alien? A piece of cake?) But together, well, what do these sentences tell us?

The blonde is attractive.

Not in an innocent sort of way, but in an aggressive, heavily sexualized way. Indeed, this is tied directly to her blondeness. So an entire raft of cultural associations are summoned up with the use of a single word—blonde. (Try it with brunette. The sentences mean something very different.)

Does the blonde have hair like straw? Is it sparse on her head? Greasy? Of course not. We can all picture this blonde's hair already, without a single extra adjective.

And what else?

Is the speaker male? Heterosexual? Yes.

Is he a pious believer in the Roman Catholic Church? Certainly not. Though he retains enough vestigial respect for that institution to make the image of the spasmodically jerking bishop a little titillating.

Does the speaker want the woman? No. There is something alienating about the "it," isn't there? (Indeed, the alienation is explicit—our speaker is actually looking at a photo of the woman, though "it" clearly refers to her, not the photo itself.) He may want blondes in general, he may want this type of woman, but he does not want this woman.

Does the speaker take his job—he's a detective—seriously? Think carefully. There are hints of both "No" and "Yes" here after all. He's joking around with his description of the blonde, of course, but he has also made a judgment about her. She's a dangerous blonde. Her beauty triggers a violent reaction from our hypothetical bishop, a person who should be immune to the charms of attractive women. The blonde doesn't even inspire our bishop to write a poem or renounce his vows or break out the Communion wine for a good stiff drink. He just loses his cool entirely and smashes a beautiful bit of his church. We're not even talking about a country parson here—a bishop is the ecclesiastical version of a cosmopolitan sophisticate.

So yes, the speaker is taking his job, and this blonde, very seriously indeed. We know this from reading the two sentences about the blonde. Chandler shows us all this, about both the subject of the sentences and their speaker, without any details being given about either of them. We don't even know very much about the bishop. But we in fact know everything.

Now, let us look at one of the worst sentences I've ever come across, this from a short story submission to *Clarkesworld,* the magazine I co-edited for two years.

> *The sergeant's jaw tightened as his eyes became wild with furry.* [sic]

The typo is hilarious, of course, but it is not as though the sentence would be any better had the writer proofread the story and corrected the word to read "fury." That's something to keep in mind about sentences—"good" sentences aren't always the grammatically correct ones, and "bad" sentences aren't simply those that pass muster with MS Word's spelling and grammar checks. This sentence could be improved very simply:

> *The sergeant's jaw tightened ~~as his eyes became wild with furry~~.*

What makes jaws tighten? Some emotional upheaval barely held in check, generally speaking. It's still not a sentence of Chandleresque quality, but it'll do. Cutting out the bit with the eyes keeps the silly verb "became" from slowing down the sentence, as well. The jaw is sufficient here. Efficiency wins the day. Like Chandler's sentence, the simple note of a jaw's movement and the rank of the person to whom it belongs, are sufficient to trigger an understanding of what is happening, and sergeants with stiff jaws are almost as popular a cultural image as the blonde bombshell.

Finally, some bad sentences from one of the most popular novels in recent memory, *The da Vinci Code*:

> A voice spoke, chillingly close. "Do not move."
>
> On his hands and knees, the curator froze, turning his head slowly.
>
> Only fifteen feet away, outside the sealed gate, the mountainous silhouette of his attacker stared through the iron bars. He was broad and tall, with ghost-pale skin and thinning white hair. His irises were pink with dark red pupils.

A few years ago a blogger named Geoffrey K. Pullum had fun dissecting these opening sentences—how did the curator freeze and move, how did a voice speak rather than a person, and manage to be both "chillingly close" and fifteen feet away? How can the elderly curator see the pale skin and irises of a silhouette? These sentences are the sort of thing that give genre fiction a bad rap amongst people who actually pay attention to words.

Pullum thinks that this is just pure bad writing, and it is, of course. But it's bad writing that goes down easy because the POV isn't that of the curator, regardless of what the quoted sentences suggested; it's that of a movie camera. The voice is "chillingly close" because the reader "sees" a close-up of the curator on the floor and hears a voice-over—thus the disembodied quality. We cut to a medium shot of the curator frozen, then when the head begins to turn, we pan to the silhouette. Then another cut to a close-up of our infamous albino monk, which is where we see his unusual coloration and even the very pinks of his eyes! Dun dun . . . DUN!

As writing, its hash. But as bestsellers are books bought by non-readers, that snippet "works" for its audience because the story is told in a manner with which they are familiar—the mode of modern Hollywood films. With the development of self-blimped cameras in the 1930s, which freed up camera movements while allowing simultaneous sound recording, we've learned a lexicon of image-meanings. Traditional film coverage and cutting is now the ingrained mode of comprehending narratives, thanks to three generations of visual media dominance. The use of written words to present a narrative is, for books like *The da Vinci Code* and too many others, a necessary evil at best. A dozen haphazard words is barely sufficient to paint a picture, and one had better not read too closely.

The use of one-sentence paragraphs and lots of simple dialogue, plus copious amounts of white space, keeps those pages turning quickly. Not only does that keep the shitty sentences from being examined till they fall apart (a nearly but not quite instantaneous event) but it takes the setting of the pace away from the reader and puts it back in the hands of the writer, or more accurately, the production staff. Again, this is just like a movie—don't blink or you'll miss something! We're in control here, you just sit back and passively receive the images.

Prose written in a cinematic style doesn't have to be bad—Joan Didion does it very well, as does, in genre, Dennis Etchison, but it sure is *easy* to generate bad writing, to not think of even how the second half of a sentence might relate to its first half, and still find a very large audience. Just write like a movie. The thinkie bits involved in reading carefully for comprehension are turned off and even atrophy, as anyone who has ever seen a "heavy reader" (five or more books a year) explode with rage over something like writing in the present tense or the use of polysyllabic words or other fancydancin' knows. For a non-reader who picks up that one big hardcover every Christmas (a gift? the airport? monkey see, monkey do?) there's nearly no hope of ever learning how to read actual sentences that make sense, never mind sentences that might even be written for their own sake, rather than to just describe "a shot."

So, after you write your sentences, read them over again, singly, or in groups of two or three. What are they saying to the reader? Is there any part of them that can be cut? Do they even make any friggin' sense? Pay attention to what you type. At least enough attention to avoid making an editor crack up laughing at you. I once had a story submitted to me that contained this sentence: "It was that calm before the storm that erupted from the home like clockwork." In another instance, someone began with his character waking up in the morning, his eyes opening with "an audible snap." I did read on just to make sure that the protagonist wasn't a robot or a freaky doll . . . .

As a fiction writer, are you taking advantage of the fact that your readers are human beings with experiences by choosing words to trigger associations and images that you don't need to spell out explicitly? If not, keep at it till you are.

[Below is one of my "Life Among the Obliterati" columns from the late lamented zine Flytrap. *One can consider dialogue a special case of the sentence, as the dialogue-sentence has specific requirements. Basically, the dialogue sentence must sound realistic—that is, it must sound like something a character would say—without actually being realistic. Realistic dialogue is rarely interesting to read, but the realistic-seeming dialogue that works in short fiction must be based on the way people speak. But how to find out how people speak? I have a few ideas . . . .]*

The Collapse

BEEN A WHILE, HASN'T IT? WELL, I'VE BEEN BUSY. I WROTE a book and a bunch of stories. I moved again, across the country from California for love, but she was depressive, and over a long, cold Vermont winter, the love leaked out of her like running sap. I was almost hospitalized with a nasty bronchial infection that kept me awake and without a drop of food for ninety-six hours. I got a $4,000 tax bill, but I was expecting a $5,300 tax bill, so it's okay. And now I may have to move again.

How do I feel? Ready to write. That's the horrid little secret of writing—everything is fodder. Even during my last plaintive blow-off discussion—when I found myself saying all those things I swore I'd never say ("But you did this to your husband two years ago; I was supposed to be different!" "I moved here just for you!") I thought, in some deep writerly corner of my mind, *remember that people do things they swear they'll never do.* What's the best way to depict a character who goes from intense love to just having it wear out, then quickly picks up someone else

39

and doesn't even realize her patterns—who is dead inside only in patches?

Same with the illness. Much of my stuff involves powers of perception, and the line between reality and mental event. Ninety-six hours awake gives one a lot of potential fodder, somatically. Do I know how someone crawling half-blind through a bog for three sultry days feels? Maybe not, but I can fake it now. I even thought, *this might make a decent column.*

Every so often, the question of experience and expertise comes up among writers. It is generally rather banal: can men write women convincingly? Can whites write black characters authentically? The answer, of course, is sure. No sweat. Not a problem.

"But!" we hear the cynic say, "how would a man know what women say when they're alone?" Easy. Listen. The world is full of thin walls and recapitulated conversations. Another experience. When visiting family members for Easter, I got to overhear a conversation between a youngish cousin and my next-door neighbor (a woman in her mid-twenties) discussing Brazilian waxing and the horrors of accidentally cutting the labia during shaving. Went right into the file. I didn't even have a brain cell to spare for being embarrassed. It was all business.

Same with race. I'm white. I lived in a predominantly black and Latino neighborhood in Jersey City for years, and during the great New York/New Jersey blackout of August 2003 I got to hear the following right outside my window. I transcribed it in the dark (I didn't even have a candle, and that, too, has been filed) and have carried the piece of paper to California and then Vermont, because it may come in handy one day. Like today:

> "I'm gonna take a walk, go see what's acting up."

"Nothing's acting up, motherfucker. Sit down. You want an orange soda? We got orange soda."

"Where'd you get orange soda?"

"We drove downtown, they got lights downtown."

"I want a Coke."

"They were out of Coke."

"How about a water?"

"We got mad water."

Some gulping sounds.

"Aaaah. I hate fucking orange soda."

"Fuck you, I like it."

"Aw man, it's too hot to fight. How come the lights are on up the block?"

"I dunno, but it makes me happy—that means they're working on it."

"Can I have some of that orange soda?"

"FUCK YOU NIGGAH . . . ah, I'm just fucking with you. I thought you didn't like it?"

"I really do like it."

People talk. People act. Writers can't help but take notes, sometimes right out there and sometimes *sub rosa*. The issue isn't the possibility of a failure, but mistakes of generalization on the part of readers who confuse *a* female/black/whatever experience with *the* female/black/whatever experience.

Another charming anecdote, ripped from my love life:

About six years ago I dated a woman who was, like myself, Greek-American. She, too, was a depressive. (Maybe I just feel the need to save people? Or maybe normal women can do better than me? I take notes on myself, too.) I encouraged her to get therapy, but she told me that she would only go if she could find a Greek-American therapist.

"Why?" I asked.

"Because of cultural issues that someone who isn't Greek wouldn't understand."

"Like what?"

"Father-daughter relationships. You know, how like Greek fathers always get very upset when their daughters start dating, and call them whores and scream and hit them. That's our culture, but for some WASP it might seem abusive."

Needless to say—especially after my references to Eastertime discussions about pussy-shaving—this was news to me, and I was as Greek as she was. My sister, aunts, cousins, other female Greek friends, etc., had never been called whores by their fathers, and some of them dated with the wild abandon that only Long Island girls with fake tans and hair higher than their ranch homes could. But a book about a Greek-American girl without a little fatherly pimp-slappin' would have rung false to this particular ex, because she was sure that her individual experiences were the general experience of her cultural milieu.

That sort of interesting denial is also something worth noting for a character, don't you think? Feel free to swipe it. I have six billion other subjects to keep track of anyway. Including myself.

[I must credit the wonderful Suzanne Kingsbury, author of the beautiful The Gospel According to Gracey, *for these additional insights into dialogue. I'm not much for writers' workshops, though I've attended one or two in the hope of learning how to run one for a few extra bucks. I enjoyed Kingsbury's exercises and even got a story out of the one I describe below. She also had an interesting approach to teaching: she only ever said positive things about people's work. Her belief was that positively reinforcing the good things would encourage writers to keep doing the good stuff, and the bad parts of their writing would eventually wither and die. I have no idea if such a thing is true—the workshop was only four weeks long, after all—but I do keep it in the back of my mind when teaching.]*

Mysteries, Secrets, and Lies

WRITING DIALOGUE SHOULDN'T BE THAT HARD. AFTER ALL, you talk to people all day, don't you? And yet, so many authors crash and burn when it comes to something as seemingly simple as having a character say something. There are any number of pitfalls, and new writers often fall into one, just to climb out and fall into the next.

The first is "teen boy" syndrome. Even though women read more widely than men and in most genres write and submit nearly as enthusiastically as men do, so many characters sound exactly like teen boys. And not very bright teen boys. The ice caps melt, and Our Hero says, "This sucks!" whether the hero is a nun in India or a polar explorer or a magical penguin. If there's a fight, someone starts it by declaring "Let's dance!" or, even worse, "You're pissing me off!" Teen boyism is especially common in first-person

43

narratives, which often take the form of an extended mono-
logue. Sheesh, are those stories awful. Luckily, outside of
some bottom-feeding horror magazines and anthologies,
no editor in his or her right mind acquires them.

At the opposite end of the spectrum is the sort of faux
elevated dialogue many fantasy writers use. No contrac-
tions, plenty of thees and thous and the occasional thus
(often used incorrectly), complex-compound sentences
that full of overstuffed clauses, and endless unintentional
portent. A favorite example from my *Clarkesworld* slush
was a line about someone's bladder, which "sings with
need" when full and its owner needs to urinate. *Just let
your Vikings pee in peace, please!*

A lot of this sort of thing is due, I believe, to late nineteenth and early twentieth century English translations
of the great myths and sagas of many lands. Though these
sagas and myths were often preserved the vernacular of
their home languages, when educated English-speakers
got their hands on 'em, they were suddenly rewritten
in language that was a bit archaic even for the period.
These translations had such a profound influence
that even today every third heroic fantasy tale comes
complete with dialogue better suited for a *Thor* comic
book, and motion pictures depicting ancient Greece and
Rome nearly inevitably roll out actors doing upper class
English accents.

Between these two extremes lies a whole spectrum of tin-
eared dialogue: scientists who sound like encyclopedia (or
worse, Wikipedia) entries; cops who end every sentence
with the words ". . . on the streets," little children who
talk like Cindy Brady, housewives who still say things like,
"Oh, you're winding me up, George!" and other spoor of a
televisual universe. Worst of all, dialogue often serves no
purpose other than to propel the narrative along. People in
bad short stories always say what they mean.

In real life, on the other hand, people only rarely say what they mean. There is an Internet Age saw about sarcasm and how difficult it is for a reader to pick up in a text. This is true, but only because a lot of Internet users are morons, and some of them are neurologically atypical. Sarcasm, false bravado, self-delusion—these can all be depicted in dialogue. And best of all, you already know how to do it, because you do it all the time in your daily life.

What you might need is to keep in mind the fact that character dialogue can serve to do more than just express in a straightforward manner what your characters are thinking and doing. Dialogue is full of mysteries (that which nobody knows), secrets (that which one character knows), and lies (that which one character knows and that other character *thinks* he or she knows). The best way I've found to integrate this into dialogue in my own stories is simply to keep it in mind. Make sure that on every page with dialogue, someone is lying, or keeping a secret, or verbally expressing (or finally resolving) a mystery of some sort.

I picked up this trick in Suzanne Kingsbury's writing workshop in 2006, and it has done well by me ever since. One of the exercises in her workshop involved simply writing a dialogue with a mystery, two secrets, and three lies. My version, reprinted below, was published as a short story in the unique venue *Postcards From Hell* (the stories were sent to subscribers on artful postcards mailed to their homes) and later performed on WXXI-FM's radio program "Fiction in Shorts." Not bad for a little exercise dashed off in five minutes in the basement of The Book Cellar in Brattleboro, Vermont. Can you find the mystery, secret, and lie in "One Thumb Up"?

[Hey, it's fiction in a nonfiction book. Don't tell anyone. Anyway, this started out as a workshop exercise, but I scored $50 for first publication rights, and then the story appeared on the radio in Central New York. It was also produced as a one-page broadsheet by Chicago's Powell's North bookstore in 2007 to celebrate a reading I did there under the auspices of Lake Forest College. I also earned $100 from the bookstore for the event, $200 from the college, and got to spend two days and nights staying in a big mansion right off campus. Don't throw anything away.]

One Thumb Up

"THAT WAS A DUMB MOVIE," I SAY AS WE LEAVE, RIGHT AFTER stepping out of earshot of the knot of enthusiastic rubes under the marquee. It's a sticky night, especially after the artificial cool of the theater, but at least it smells like the world again instead of buttered chemistry. "If you put that much rat poison in someone's drink, they'll smell it, taste it after one sip. Nobody's going to drink a whole jelly jar full of Kool-Aid and vodka that tastes like that."

"Really?" Barb says, her voice light and suddenly interested. She hadn't liked the movie either, but stuck it out for me. Barb's a walker-outer, but I'll sit through any piece of crap I spent ten bucks on, so we'd stayed. "That's a relief."

I laugh. She doesn't. We get to the car. Finally, I say "Huh?"

"Well, I worry."

"About being poisoned?"

"Yes," she says. "It's one of those ways to die, you know. An unexpected way, so I try to expect it so it won't happen. How do you think you're going to die?"

47

"Old age, heart attack . . . ." I say, listing the usual.

"No." Barb's upset now. Again. She'd been upset during the movie, too, after I hissed at her when she tugged on my arm to go. She sees my look and backtracks a bit. "Not for me, anyway." She starts the car and speaks offhandedly except for the puff of breath she knocks against her bangs to get her hair out of her eyes. She looks in the rearview mirror. "I don't see myself getting old." The car rumbles under me. "You don't think someone might ever try to poison you?"

"No, who would?"

"Anybody."

"Would you?"

"No, of course not."

"Why do you think you're going to be poisoned?" I ask.

"It's been on my mind a lot," she says. She's quiet for a moment, maybe envisioning gagging and keeling over, hands to her own throat, Froot Loops and splatters of white milk everywhere, or maybe she's just concentrating on pulling out of the lot.

"Or being shot by someone, maybe a stray bullet," she starts. "Or the furnace blows up, or I fall down the steps and break my neck. Well, that might just paralyze me and I'd starve to death in the time it would take for anyone to miss me." Great, she'd been compiling a list.

"Or," she says as we pull onto Route 9, to get to the expressway, "just having that crazy urge when you're about to go under an overpass, to just twist the wheel and veer left hard, and smash yourself into the concrete."

"What? You think about that? I mean . . . a lot? You gotta be kiddin'."

"Why?" Barb's voice is light again, but with confusion, not relief. "Don't you?"

"No!" I say. "I'm sure nobody else does either. Not normal people anyway. That's like a sign of severe depression or something, to be so obsessed with death."

"Oh, what do you know?" she says. "You don't even drive." Then she hits the gas hard.

[Short stories, particularly in commercial fiction, tend to have a lot of scene breaks. You know, a few blank lies followed by a new scene. Well, one hopes a new scene. The speculative genres—SF, fantasy, and horror—are chock full of information about the setting, and crime/mystery stories often cut to another scene after a character comes up with a plan or arrives at some realization. Scene breaks are thus very important in short fiction, as the usual tricks of the novelist—extended "infodumps" for SF, prologues in fantasy and horror, extended dialogues between characters in crime/mystery—are unavailable to the short story writer who wants to avoid writing something too long for a magazine and too short for a standalone book . . . . The problem is that scene breaks are very prone to misuse. Scene breaks all but invite an editor to stop reading at the break, so be sure you use them only when necessary and proper.]

What is a Scene Break,
He Asked Rhetorically?

#

SO THERE WE WERE, READING DOZENS AND DOZENS OF STORIES, and suddenly it became very easy to reject many of them, as they had a tell that let us know that we as readers were not in sure hands. Many, many stories we'd seen recently abused the scene break.

If a scene break were a physical item, it would be an 800-pound gong.

You don't want to sound a gong this large all the time. You'll deafen people, interrupt their conversations, annoy the hell out of everyone, and drown out any other instruments that might be playing. You certainly don't want to sound this gong again while the sound of the first is still ringing in the ears of the audience.

A scene break is thus primarily useful when the break is profound and signaling it is thus very important. When switching from one story to another, or if many years pass, or if many things happen off-page between the scenes in between which you are inserting a break, then yes, of course use a scene break. Auctorial intrusions and fabulist asides are also welcome to be placed between # and #.

When the break is less profound, do not use a scene break. A scene break does not mean "And then . . ." nor does it mean "Meanwhile."

Also, a special note for first-person narratives: individuals rarely speak in scene breaks. In fact, if you speak in scene breaks, please report to the nearest research university, as I think there might be a linguistics thesis in you for some lucky grad student.

In the stories I've read recently, scene breaks are abused frequently, and often in the same way. For example, there's this:

> [the whole history of the fucking universe, especially intertribal conflicts and climactic change of some sort, plus a little child sent out into the world on a portentous errand]

> #

> [Little child, now an adult, taking a dump in the woods.]

This is wrong because not only do you not need the break, you generally don't need the exegesis. Short stories aren't teeny tiny novels with a prologue and then some stuff that happens.

Then there's this one:

[Some ass hears the alarm, gets up in the morning, pulls on his pants, excretes]

#

[Twenty seconds later, in the car, the radio has some important news]

Forget the tedium of starting with your character waking up in the morning, there's no need to break here at all. Just put him in the car.

Another goodie:

[OMG SOME CRAZY-ASS THING JUST HAPPENED]

#

["Hello, friend" says the person to whom some crazy-ass thing just happened, "I have a paragraph to repeat to you, nearly word for word."]

Ugh.

But the worst is this version:

[Hello! I am character!]

#

[and then . . .]

#

[and then . . .]

#

[FLASHBACK TO THE FIRST 'and then']

#

[some confusing stuff]

#

[epilogue explaining what happened to the character during the confusing stuff]

Asides: How To Use 'Em

I would make a distinction between a line break, a scene break, and a chapter break, even if they all serve the same purpose—to skip over something, recharge the reader, and signal a transition. A line break (or an extra line break; one more carriage return) is a mild transition. Putting in a # or other doodad is a signal of a greater break. A chapter break is a greatest of all. Take this line in an entirely hypothetical story:

"You'll never take me alive, imperialist pigs!" Joseph shouted, raising his AK.

Now, two carriage returns:

Later that night, in prison, Joseph tried to enjoy his salisbury steak.

A bit of a transition. Not too much. Now with a doodad #:

At Joseph's funeral, his son, Joseph Jr. vowed revenge on America.

Now with a portentous chapter break.

II.

Harvey always enjoyed Martyr's Day. The government not only outfitted him with slightly longer leg irons for the holiday, it also let him eat all the pigeons he could kill as part of their statuary protection program.

Seeing that all the busts of Joseph—Leader, Founder, and Father of all of us—made a more popular toilet than anything else, Harvey wondered if there wasn't something in the way the bronze of Joseph's bald head gleamed under the sun.

See? Link tends to write longer stories and have pretty profound changeups when she uses chapter breaks. It's not only a deep breath for her, it's often a radical change of thematic position, even if it's not a change of subject or speaker. Read your stories again and I think you'll see what I mean.

Give the scene breaks a rest, folks. My ears are still bleeding from the last fifty hammers to the gong.

[This 2008 piece was especially amusing to me because my time at Mo*Con led directly to my return to the Midwest later that year for another convention: Context of Columbus, Ohio. I had just wrapped up the anthology Haunted Legends, *which I co-edited with Ellen Datlow. At Context I met a writer who was in the same writing group as John Mantooth, whose story I'd acquired for the anthology. He remarked that he was thrilled for his friend, but was also surprised, as Mantooth had gone against the advice of many members of the writing group—they'd recommended an ending that would have "neatly wrapped up the story" by having the main character burn a very important object.*

I had to laugh because I'd enjoyed the story greatly and was happy to pass it on to Ellen. I'd spent the entire time of my reading thinking to myself, This is great. God, I hope he doesn't ruin the story by having the main character set everything on fire at the end. An editor is always ready to reject—every sentence is a fight between acceptance and rejection, all the way to the end. Don't punt on the endings. The most heartbreaking of the stories I've rejected earned their rejection slips on the last paragraph.]

How to End a Story

WARNING: EDDIE CAMPBELL, IN *HOW TO BE AN ARTIST*, HIS wonderful autobiographical comic, explains that the advice within should be taken as to how to be an artist successfully, not how to be a successful artist. All advice here is the same. This is how to write a good ending, not how to write an ending that will make the story saleable. There actually is a difference, which I will discuss at the end of this.

And now, another anecdote—this past weekend, I was at Mo*Con, and at Mo*Con was a Celtic rock band called Mother Grove who played an extended set. I'm not much for diddly-diddly music, but it was good and fun and their fiddle player was cute so I stuck around. For most of it. Mother Grove, like many artists who are given free rein, ruined themselves by playing too long. I went to bed before they covered Public Enemy's "Don't Believe the Hype," which should have been how they ended the set an hour before. Then the experience would have been much better, though shorter. Actually, though is the wrong word—because it would have been shorter.

That's how you end a story: with a) a bang and b) leaving the reader hungry for more. The bang is easy enough, but what about hunger?

Too many stories make one of two errors—they cop out on the implications of the story or exhaust the reader. Both serve to stop the story rather than end it; both fail to leave the reader hungry for more.

The most obvious cop-out is the well-known "it was all a dream" ending, which erases the implications by erasing the plot. There are others—wiping out the protagonist for ill-considered reasons, and having any evidence of the revelations of the story left obscure or hidden or just unstated are others.

I read two stories in the *Clarkesworld* slush, one good, one not. The good one was quite exciting; it was one of those times where, as I was reading, I said to myself, "I'm buying this if he doesn't mess up the ending."

And he messed up the ending. The story involved a weird discovery of a new world (in broad strokes, to hide what story this is) and Person A telling Person B all about it, and then saying, "Well, see ya!" and then diving into that new world. Person B worried that he might be questioned by the police, so dove into the new world too. The end.

Awful.

The implication of the story is the discovery of the new world—what will it mean, how might it change things, what's Person B gonna do now! By eliminating Person B, the implications of the story are eliminated. The story is not ended, but rather *stopped,* as there is no pleasure to be gained by contemplating the story or its thematic and mimetic implications anymore, unless you ignore the ending. Indeed, I've daydreamed about several alternative endings for this story, just because the first 97 percent of it was so interesting. But, as a reader, I don't want to do the work of fixing the ending to allow for these post-reading daydreams and musings, I want the story to actively inform them.

This story didn't leave us hungry for more because of a bad dessert that upset our collective stomach. We're full and bloated and don't want to ever eat again. Bad.

The second story was just the sort of bad story tyros write. Time traveling guy buttonholes a scientist, says he has something for Mr. Science (the "Huh? "No!" "Impossible!" guy for this particular dialogue-driven story), and that thing is . . . a Presidential assassin. Mr. Science says, "Oh boy, I've got some questions for you." The end.

Awful.

What are the implications of a long-dead man coming to the narrative present? Well, the "questions" for one thing. What to do with him afterward, for another. What he may think of the modern world is another. Is he gonna shoot somebody else? That's a good one, too! Nuffin'. In this the reader is not left hungry for more because we didn't get to eat in the first place. That whole story is the first line of a real story.

The end of a story should connect back to the beginning in some way that makes the beginning more interesting and gives the reader something to linger on afterward. This is why it's not a great idea to title your story after its last line, why ending with protagonist suicides and murders is fraught with the peril of tedium, why tying up every single loose end is not a good idea.

A good ending either takes a step back or pushes one step ahead. Let that last bit of awe or confusion follow the reader, or the final tragedy or triumph echo a bit after the protagonist experiences it. Leave that ragged edge at the end, that line—"Gazing up into the darkness I saw myself as a creature driven and derided by vanity; and my eyes burned with anguish and anger."

This brings us to readerly exhaustion. What if our young hero in the line above explained how he went home and cried all night and his mother asked, boredly, "What's wrong, dear" and he couldn't bring himself to say what was bothering him because he was just a kid so instead he said that someone made a mean face at him while he was at the Araby and then, later, while on the commode he wondered why he had said such a thing and so he decided to write a diary entry about it, which is what you are reading right now?

Awful.

Don't pave over the implications of the story by repeating the ending—that great moment of revelation above—three or four times. We'll get it. We're not dumb. Don't streeeeetch out the story's ending to make sure some neat sentence was included or to hammer home exactly what the reader should experience. Step back. Leave the reader wanting to know more about the character, the circumstance; leave room for that post-reading daydream.

Aside: Oh, and for the love of God, if you're writing a first-person story, think about how that character might actually sit down and tell the story. If you were attacked by a dragon at the grocery store and called your friend right afterward, would you say "Guess what, I was just attacked by a dragon. What happened was . . ." or "Guess what, I just went to the grocery store! And I bought eggs, and pork chops, and I stepped in some gum in the parking lot and I thought back to the time I went to Maine for the long weekend and rolled up my pants to wade in the surf and then a dragon attacked me. Oh well, talk to you later"? In these stories, the major implication is that the story itself is a told thing, and the ending must reflect the reason for its telling, just as the beginning must reflect the reason for the listener to pay attention.

But but but, what about tying everything up in a neat little bow and leaving nothing unsaid or undone? No. That's common enough bad advice, but it is not advice that serves the story. Rather it serves the political economy of popular magazines as they existed in the first half of the last century. Magazine circulations are a function of print run and sales, but only a function of the same. There is a multiplier effect, the "pass around" of someone leaving the magazine behind on a table, bus, or in an office, and someone else looking at it. Magazine content is designed to be disposable, so that the artifact can be freed up to be examined by more people, thus exposing the ads—and the magazine itself—to a wider audience. The magazine as an object is its own best advertisement.

What did this mean for fiction content? Essentially, it means that the stories in these popular magazines had to resist rereading or being interesting enough for the buyer to hang on to the issue, or rip out the pages (and associated ads) to look at again. The "well-tied bow" ending is a design feature to make you forget about the story and let the magazine go.

These days, however, the popular magazines no longer carry fiction and content is all going online. That means that the "pass around" is dead; modern audiences need to be "pulled" toward content, they cannot have it "pushed" at them. Thus, a story has to have such an effect on a reader as to make him or her want to share that experience by sending the story to friends, or by broadcasting it via links on a blog, email, Twitter, etc. Only by following through on the implications of the story, and only to the extent that the reader wants more, can this happen.

Contemporary editorial advice is still informed by the pulp era, when stories needed to be easily disposable. However, the economy of the story is changing under the feet of the current generation of editors. If you want to be good, leave the ragged edge. You may not sell your stories immediately—not until the current crop of well-entrenched editors dies, perhaps—but when they do sell in the new online environment, they will be well-regarded.

So end your stories, don't just stop them.

An Aside: Murder Everything Else

Dr. Henry Gee wrote me today to tell me that a story I sold to *Nature* in the summer (of 2007) will appear in the Nov 1 issue. He also wrote "I know I've probably said it before, but the deciding factor in your story was your decision to include the word Weltanschauung. There's a conspiracy theory in there, all by itself. Ol' Goethe knew a thing or two . . . ."

So there you go!

Or, perhaps more to the point, stories that stand out and thus get published are not just good—my story was apparently engaging enough for Gee to read through, as the thrilling word appears close to the very end—but must contain that which other stories lack. It can be a word or turn of phrase, an interesting concept or twist, a snatch of dialogue—*Donnie Darko* is made by the rejoinder "Why are you wearing that stupid human suit?"—an unusual or interesting setting, or virtually anything that doesn't boil down to miserable sameness. Slush has a consistency, just like its snowy namesake, and you need a little hard hunk of . . . something in order to stand out.

You know that old saying, "Murder your darlings"? One time, try the opposite: keep the darling, murder everything else, and write a new story around that jewel.

[And now, I dare critique Shakespeare. Well, not really. The point here is twofold—don't overpolish, which is advice easy enough to accept for most writers, because polishing one's work is tedious. The second point is trickier: flaws are what make a piece worth rereading. What is worth rereading is worth publishing and worth reprinting.]

The Ragged Edge

I'M TEACHING A COURSE AT GRUB STREET INC., A WRITING center here in Boston, called "Popular Fiction: Writing the Page-Turner." Despite the title, I have a few students with more literary inclinations. One is so literary, in fact, that he won't write anything. I had instructed them that they could only bring in completed work—material with a beginning, middle, and end (though not necessarily in that order). I simply didn't want to spend class time brainstorming a climax for some half-formed short story, or someone to hand in everything they'd written of a novel so far. You know, three and a half chapters. Our friend, let's call him James Joyce, took "completed" to mean "finished," and was thus paralyzed. Nothing is ever, ever finished until every phoneme is perfectly aligned in a matrix of liguisto-thematic purity so quintessentially perfect that our mere brains can scarcely comprehend what we're reading. Indeed, our minds register the material as blank pages, except for a few doodles.

I can't say I ever understood this quest for perfection, which is self-evidently quixotic at any rate and of course just a neurotic response to the possibility of failure. Perfect stuff isn't even likely all that much fun to read, even if it does exist. Good writers always leave us something to mull over, a flaw to mess with. Here's an example from Shakespeare's Sonnet XVIII:

> Shall I compare thee to a Summer's day?
> Thou are more lovely and more temperate:
> Rough winds do shake the darling buds of May,
> And Summer's lease hath all too short a date

"Temperate," eh? When was the last time you called your lover temperate? Oh, he's great. Very temperate. More temperate than summer. You know, like spring, really? Which is less good than summer, except when it comes to temperance. So I really am contrasting him to a summer's day, and comparing him to a spring one. Anyway, I love him. He rubs my feet after a long day of treading the boards at the Globe and running from my many creditors.

In addition to making little sense, "temperate" is just a weak adjective. Almost by definition it suggests moderation rather than passion. Further, to read the poem correctly, you must pronounce the word "temp-er-ATE," which may well have been the pronunciation in Shakespeare's day, but which falls a bit flat here in 2011.

Perfection cannot be bound by time, after all. Poetic license is fine, but license works better when the first instance of that "B"-rhyme is pronounced normally, thus signaling the use of license in the fourth line. However, that would lead to the fourth line sounding like this when read aloud:

> And Summer's lease hath all too short a "debt"

This line, with that last word, would thus mean just enough to mean almost nothing. And this is Shakespeare, the greatest writer in the English language. James Joyce, of course, is second. (The real James Joyce, not the kid in my class.) So I explained this, and explained how imperfections are not only inevitable, but can be a tool. Think of the ellipses of Celine, or Kerouac's tortured sentences, or even the purposeful confusion generated by leaving out dialogue tags for an extended period. All these things make the reading process more difficult, purposefully, to make a specific demand on the reader's attention. Work that is too obviously and highly polished becomes soulless rather than elegant.

It was a pretty good speech, I thought. (Not perfect, of course.)

Anyway, James Joyce dropped out of class right after that. It's almost a demographical inevitability—a male student who is younger than I am and who just graduated from a prestigious school and course of study (e.g. Harvard business, MIT engineering) and who comes into my class will freak out at the in-class writing assignments, refuse to hand in stuff to the workshop, and will then vanish. There are some people who just cannot comprehend the possibility that the norms of their own field do not translate in an uncomplicated fashion to writing. And learning something new, even about good old perfect Shakespeare, well, that's just too hard for an engineering genius or a business school prodigy or a hotshot associate attorney.

My writing advice for people who really do worry about having perfectly polished work stands: be less temperate. Keep those ragged edges, and learn how to use them.

[I'm not big on revision, actually. Though of course many people like to quote Truman Capote's critique of Jack Kerouac— "That's not writing, that's typing"—the fact is that lots of writers manage to work and publish without significant revision between drafts. And we're not just talking pulp hacks, either. Edward Albee famously doesn't revise, and within the fantasy genre, Caitlin R. Kiernan doesn't revise either. This isn't to say that they don't correct typos or occasionally cut a sentence, or add one, here and there. What these writers don't do, and what I don't do, is work through multiple drafts in order to find the structure and tone of a piece. Unfortunately, there's no way to teach this knack—it does seem more prevalent amongst less commercial writers, though.

As an editor and teacher, I am a proponent of revision. Here's a short essay on the piece of advice I give most often.]

When In Doubt, Cut It Out

HAVING READ A VERY LARGE NUMBER OF AWKWARDLY SHAPED stories in my roles as an editor and leader of workshops, I am beginning to wonder whether workshops should exist at all. I've found that I'm more likely to get a story that just stops for several paragraphs to make way for some tedious explanation (of magic, of some scientific or legal principle, of the inner workings of some character's mind) from writers who participate in workshops. And these are generally pieces that have been revised. What I believe is happening is that the workshop process is actually making the stories worse.

"I didn't get . . ." is how many people begin their critiques of a story under review in a workshop, after all. I didn't get why Theodore was so upset. I don't understand how a ghost can travel between cell phones as voice mail, but can get stuck in an answering machine if its unplugged. I don't know what pyrotechnic safety switches are or how they are used on a manned capsule atop a rocketship. I don't know why Julia used a knife to kill Frederick instead of the gun she'd found on page 3. Our writer, eager to improve his or her story, goes home with all these notes and puts in a few paragraphs explaining how ectoplasm works, or about how Theodore was touched by his parish priest as a child, or has a scientist explain to another scientist why it is ever-so-important that a circuit be cut off immediately in the capsule, or adds a whole page of Julia reading a mystery novel so that her knowledge of powder burns can be shared with the reader. And so the story grows a tumor of explanation. It slows down. Readers understand what's going on, but at the cost of being entertained.

In science fiction, the material needed just to explain what's going on is often presented in big multi-page long blocks cleverly called "infodumps." Of course, the other genres have their infodumps as well—mysteries often have long asides about police procedure, for example, and romances present the reveries of their protagonists to provide information about the emotional states of the characters. There's nothing wrong with infodumps; the trick is to handle them properly. Many of the old routines are obvious to readers these days. Staff briefings or conversations between an ignoramus and a wise person, a bite of food that summons forth a flood of memories, the radio or TV report that just happens to be about the serial killer on the loose, you've likely read them all, and you've certainly seen them all at the movies. In some books, especially hard SF and historical fiction, infodump may not even be disguised as narrative—it just gets plopped right in.

The infodump need not be boring. That there are a large number of books about science, boating, history, etc., and hundreds of thousands of magazines and newspapers that cover various nonfiction topics. A proper infodump simply needs to have the information the reader needs, and no more. Fiction is all about giving the reader all the information he or she is expecting, and even some more than that, but not too much. Do not simply cut out infodumps.

Instead, when you write, make sure that your narrative universe isn't overly complex. Don't expand infodumps and other bits of exposition in a story to make sure that every workshop attendee, "beta reader," or relative gets every concept in your story. Instead, if there is something confusing or that needs too much explanation in your story, just eliminate it entirely. What cannot be explained succinctly in a short story should just be cut.

["Fantatwee" is certainly a contemporary problem in fantasy, but virtually every genre of short fiction has its own version. In crime/mystery, we could call this sort of second-order genre "fauxoir," in horror "horrah," in SF good ol' "skiffy." Every genre has tropes, and every genre at this point has enough tropes that semi-literate individuals can more or less sew together several of them to make a sort-of story. This use of tropes is far different from the simple writing of pastiche or parody in that the end never rises to the level of the old stuff being ripped off. Tanith Lee and Neil Gaiman's retelling of the Snow White story found something new in that story; in fantatwee, there will never be anything new.

This think piece about the nature of debased genre writing appeared in my blog, and is reprinted here because science fiction literary critic Farah Mendlesohn used it as part of her course reader at the university at which she teaches. If it's good enough for college kids, it's good enough for you. Even if you don't write fantasy, you should contemplate the tropes of the genres in which you do write, and use them wisely rather than as a semi-comical crutch. Are you writing a mystery, or are you writing about how much you enjoy reading mysteries? Are you writing a horror story, or a love letter to horror stories . . . or even worse, horror movies! Keep this in mind. Genre implies a certain amount of repetition of themes and set pieces, but needs more from its new writers than regurgitation.]

What is Fantatwee?

KARL MARX'S APHORISM, "RELIGION . . . IS THE OPIATE OF the people" is often expressed without the ellipsis, as if that were his complete theory-cum-denunciation of religion, or even an accurate quote. However, Marx was aware of—and hardly the first to be aware of—the dual nature and purpose of religion. While reactionary and a tool of social control, it is also an attempt to deal with the alienation of the human essence. Religion is not only the opiate of the people, it is the "sigh of the oppressed," the "hope of a hopeless world," and the "soul of soulless conditions," to fill that which the ellipsis omits. Opiates can be useful, occasionally, as anyone who has ever visited in a dentist will know. Opiates, however, are ultimately palliatives, not treatments of underlying conditions.

The Marx quote, both what it actually says and how it is usually presented so that it appears to glibly suggest that religion is just a racket, comes to mind when I read *Clarkesworld Magazine* slush. We receive a lot of stories that I have begun to call "fantatwee"—a portmanteau of twee and fantasy. I haven't published any, but, if you're very curious, a fair number of them end up in *Fantasy Magazine*. Fantatwee is fantasy with an ellipsis; the implications of the story and its themes are omitted so that the act of reading—and, I suspect, writing—is mostly purely palliative.

There are two major families of fantatwee, the first being the retold unreconstructed fairy tale. These stories recite a fairy tale, generally something from Grimm and very, very often a retelling of Snow White (and sometimes Snow White with vampires). The second type of fantatwee are stories about how awesome fantasy stories are.

At the risk of engaging in a little biocrit, many young people find solace in fantasy stories. It's escapism, which isn't all that dirty a word. Plenty of realist literature is escapist as well—one simply escapes into the world of aspirational middle-class problems in which one's relations drink and then sit on a sofa to weep as opposed to drinking and then balling up their fists to smash your head in because the rice was burnt. There was escapism in the Gulags too. Escapism is not, by itself, an evil. It is no surprise that these young readers, when they grow up, attempt to recreate the joyous bits of their childhoods by writing stories with this same escapist quality.

Unfortunately, fantatwee is all about second-order escapism. Many great stories have elements of escapism, but also a twist of a thematic screw that lets the reader know that not everything is strawberries and cream. Hard choices get made. Misery abides. In the film version of *Return of the King*, Frodo may have had a big pillow fight with his friends and then moped about the house for a bit. In the book, he was a shattered man, utterly alienated from his communitarian society. That's what you get for saving the world from doom.

Fantatwee leaves out the shell shock. In the fairy tale mode, the jagged edges of fairy tales are filed off and replaced with a faux threat—Snow White with fangs, a few more mentions of blood, that sort of thing. But there's no terror, no threat of the horrid arbitrariness that lies at the intersection of fairyland and early modernity. The story isn't renovated or explored or undermined. Instead, what enjoyment there is in the reading of it is the stuff of bedtime: "Once upon a time . . . the end." "Read it again, mama!" Nothing drives the story but the prior existence of the story; the new version's theme is nothing more than "Hey, remember this old story that used to mean something? Well, it still used to."

The second type of fantatwee is often contemporary, and the fantastic is an intrusion, though a very welcome one from the monotony of being on the right-hand side of the developmental bell curve. Protagonists are awkward, shy, sans libido and also bereft of any negative traits. Unlike the young nerds who populate Earth-1—and we were certainly arrogant, pissy, often annoying, quick to take offense, so terrified of humiliation that we humiliated ourselves and blamed others—these protagonists are just the sweetest ol' things, perfectly misunderstood by the barbarians around them and perfectly loved by the author. All this sweet little kid needs is a revelation of how uncomplicatedly awesome the world of fantasy is. Wish-fulfillment, power fantasies, the conflation of escapism and escape, all of these are unalloyed positive goods presented on a silver tray in fantatwee.

In addition to being thematically weak, this set of stories is the stuff of indulgence; all those neat treats on the silver tray have bites taken from them and the teeth indentations seem to match the mouth of the author. I'm reminded not only of Marx's line about the opiate of the people here, but that funny headline from *The Onion* that went something like "High School Shooter Finds That Bloody Massacre Solved All His Problems" . . . except a story with that plot would be interesting. At least the protagonist did a little protagging, rather than just waiting for God The Author to bless the righteously meek with dragons and castles. Your prize for being picked on in junior high school is a magic wand and a green button that lets you touch boobs.

What is a good story? A good story is one that is thematically interesting enough to be reread without being understood exactly the same way the second time. Fantatwee is opium without treatment. Once you come to, you still are the same ol' person you were before, with the usual pains in the usual spots.

Interestingly, the edit of Marx's aphorism moves him to the right, not the left. Though "harder" on religion, the expurgated quote more closely aligns with the mainstream of Enlightenment thought, which saw the public cults as nothing but a clerical conspiracy. Fantatwee also often presents itself as something new—knowing reduxes of fairy tales, or winking exploration of fantasy tropes and even the act of reading fantasy—but in the end is just the same old wine in a not-very-new bottle. Stories about the magic of storytelling are not only not magic, they're barely even stories.

This is not to say that retold fairy tales cannot be thematically deep, or that fantasy stories about fantasy stories are just so much soma. The point is to find the problem that exists somewhere inside the fairy tale, or in the act of being a kid who wants to escape the mundane, and explore that problem. Don't ignore the problem, or become so enamored with the fantasia that the problem is denied entirely.

Aside: What Is A Good Story?

I propose a moratorium on the phrase, said by editors of venues who publish short stories (magazines, anthologies, collections, etc.), "I just want good stories."

The reason I think editors should no longer say this is because it is a lie and a transparent one. Editors clearly do not just want good stories.

For one thing, most stories aren't any good at all. When was the last time you read an issue of a magazine containing several stories and said "Wow, these are all good stories!" Or an anthology? Or a collection? Most stories are just there to take up space and to "satisfice" (my favorite portmanteau) some perceived need, and that need can be to fill 256 pages or to make sure there is one story about a spaceship in each issue or because the story was written by someone who used to be famous or because it was the best of a bad, bad lot and the editor has no idea how to cultivate a slush pile or solicit actual work and the thing is due in five days.

I don't want good stories. I want stories of a certain type. If all I wanted to do was publish good stories, I'd not bother with slush or any of that stuff, but just take a story from the Chekhov archive and paste it up. All the stories in that archive are better than anything I've ever published, or written. I could choose stories from that archive at random and wildly exceed the mission to "just choose good stories" better than every SF/F/H editor ever, combined. Hell, I could publish "Araby" every single month, and every single month *Clarkesworld* would feature THE GREATEST SHORT STORY EVER WRITTEN IN ENGLISH.

Wouldn't you look at a magazine if each month the single best story ever written was in it?

I don't want good stories. I want good stories of a certain length. I'm not going to publish a novella on an online venue, even if other editors think that sort of thing is a good idea. I'm not going to publish a story that takes the form of four interconnected haiku, even if other editors think that sort of thing is a good idea. I'm not going to publish these types of stories regardless of their quality.

I don't want good stories. I want good stories that have certain plots and themes. I do not want any stories, for example, about a woman stitching a stillborn child's corpse to a fish's tail, or about a post-Singularity being who is lonely, or of a Filipino goblin writing a letter to another member of the local Communist Party. I've already run those stories. Even if the stories I receive with those plots in the future are better than the ones I've already published, I don't want them. I want something else.

I don't want good stories. I want good stories written by authors with whom I am comfortable having a business relationship. If you tell me to go fuck a porcupine and then send me the greatest story since "Araby," I still don't want it. If you send me "Araby" and insist that you wrote it, I really, really don't want it. If you send me a story about

Captain Kirk, I don't want that either. If you send me a story featuring my own submission guidelines, I don't want that.

I don't want good stories. I want great writing with no story, good stories with great writing, wonderful anti-stories with poor writing, nifty ideas on silver platters, stories that depend on having read some other story to make any sense at all, stories that nobody will think are good until three days after they are read, stories that couldn't have been written before 1969, stories that will never be written again after 9/11/2001, mood pieces, monologues, atmospheric effects, grand tours, minute examinations of places I've never been, thinly-veiled autobiographies, grocery lists, liner notes of records never pressed, stories about pro wrestling that only people well-versed in kayfabe will fully understand, stories written as if "story" were some weird new thing that nobody ever heard of, etc.

So, please, stop. "I just want good stories" is a lie. And if it's not a lie, it's some sort of willful failure of self-awareness. Not a good sign in anyone with thumbs and a big forehead.

[Another Flytrap *essay, this one covering two subjects I don't know very much about: selling out and selling a pair of novels to a major publisher for a very nice advance.* Starve Better's *emphasis is on short subjects, but many people wish to be novelists and (foolishly) see short stories and short nonfiction as a stepping stone to writing popular novels.*

Sadly, writing short fiction doesn't necessarily develop the skills needed to write a successful novel. Some of the reasons we've covered already, others are covered below. Are you ready to get a book deal only by writing several books first? By promising to write another book in perhaps a few months, even if it took years to write your first book? By "throwing away" the novel you really wanted to publish in order to spend your time on something more commercial? Meet Paul Tremblay, novelist, from this interview I conducted in 2008.]

Way to Sell Out, Paulie!

AH, "SELLING OUT." WOULD-BE WRITERS ARE OFTEN extremely worried about selling out—what are they going to do when confronted with a big ol' check by an oily editor who only wants a few changes to the magnum opus. Of course, the real worry is this: all the writers who are published are so eager to sell out that the price of doing so has declined significantly in real dollars. The average advance for a first novel is just about $5,000, just as it was twenty years ago. Twenty years ago, by the way, a year of college at my alma mater, SUNY Stony Brook, was $1350.

Then, just a few days ago, my friend Paul Tremblay contacted me to share with me some good news: he sold two novels to Henry Holt for an advance of $75,000. The second one is not only not yet written, it wasn't yet even conceived of when the deal was struck. Paul, who has had small press collections (*Compositions For Young and Old*, *City Pier*) and who edited fiction for both *ChiZine* and *Fantasy Magazine*, agreed to talk to me about how he wrote, and sold, his first novel.

NM: So, what's your book about?

PT: It's called *The Little Sleep*. Mark Genevich is a narcoleptic private detective living in South Boston. The book has fun with the usual PI conventions, while poking around in the nature of reality. What's real, what's a construct? And hopefully it's funny in the right places.

NM: You're primed to be an overnight sensation. How many novels have you written, how many partials, how many agents did you solicit before getting one, and how many rejections for your books do you have?

PT: I have written 4.5 novels. 2.5 are dead and buried. I retained my agent Stephen Barbara (Donald Maas) on the strength of a novel I wrote in 2003. That novel accrued (safe estimate) over 200 agent rejections. Most of the rejections included the line, "this is funny and original, but we can't sell this." Sadly, they were right. Stephen couldn't sell it. The editors, about twenty in total, rejected the book and said the same thing. "Nice work, but we can't sell this."

We decided to stop shopping this particular novel in February of 2007. I spent the next two months researching and plotting *The Little Sleep* and spent the rest of the spring and summer writing the novel. The pitch and sale of this novel was fast (three weeks), but yeah, it was a long overnight.

NM: You're living not only the dream, but also the cliché: a big-money deal—$75,000 advance for a first novel and a second not yet even conceived of—but only if you change the ending and write a sequel. How do you feel about that?

PT: The ending change turned out to be not all that drastic. I ostensibly added a chapter, which, I'm happy to say, works within the spirit of the "original" ending. I may even grudgingly agree (grudge, grudge, grudge) that the added chapter makes for a better ending.

The second question is harder to answer. If you asked me three weeks ago, I would've told you there was no way I was going to write a sequel. Now, I'm geared up for it. Hopefully I'm up to the challenge of writing a book that won't feel like a tack-on, that will use the same character and still be fresh and say something new. But I'd be lying if I said the second book doesn't make me nervous.

NM: Stephen King has probably been the most popular author in the world for three decades, and yet he's still quite defensive about his place in the literary pantheon: his whining speech at the National Book Awards, etc. Then there are thousands of small-press authors, of which you were one until this week, and many find the idea of "selling out" to be just awful. So, any new insights from your leap across the chasm?

PT: Not a whole lot of insights yet. We're just getting started with the revision schedule and deadlines, etc. I will freely admit that I wrote *The Little Sleep* with the idea that it would sell. I knew, even before writing the book, that it had a hook, and Stephen was confident it had a hook and a plot (those editors do love their plots). That said, after the initial concept and plot outline, I approached *Sleep*'s actual composition as I have any other story or work of mine. I didn't dumb it down or hide the ugliness and darkness that I think makes up much of my small press work.

NM: Why did you want a book that sold? I know that may sound like a stupid question, but I mean, do you want to quit teaching school? Buy a big car? Purchase some better-behaved children?

PT: First, I do like the book, quite a bit. And I actually wrote the first chapter before I had acquired my agent with *Phobia* (the doomed novel). But I stopped writing *Sleep* because I was still trying to sell *Phobia* (which featured a character who suffered from debilitating fears) and I didn't think it was prudent to write a follow-up to *Phobia* with another character with a disease. So when *Phobia* was declared dead, It was good to go back to *Sleep*.

Anyway, to actually answer your question . . . I want my books to be read by the largest audience I can sustain. I love teaching, but I do want to write full-time. Now, since I've (many would argue, foolishly so!) established a middle-class lifestyle with employee-paid health insurance, house, kids, and the like, writing as a gig to pay the bills I've made for myself is going to be tough. Even with the great and exciting Holt deal, I won't be quitting teaching for a while.

NM: Do you think that unsalable book will be more salable now? That the magazines that rejected your short work will now be more open to it?

PT: I have no solid or scientific basis for conclusion here, but my gut instinct, based on reactions I've received from some folks already, is that I will have an easier time placing short stories. Not that I expect or demand such a thing. But maybe I should demand it!

As far as novels go, the fear is I'll have a harder time placing stand-alone novels. I do have a novel that I'm revising titled *Swallowing a Donkey's Eye*, which is set in my *City Pier* world, a dark satire/genre/dystopian stew. We'll see what happens with that book when we show it around next year or so.

NM: Do you have plans, even psychological ones, for the possibility of the books not coming close to earning out their advance and you ending up being unable to publish with large commercial publishers ever again under your own name?

PT: I'm still riding the post-closing high right now, but I've considered that scenario, of course. I'm sure I'll consider it more as the publication date approaches. I'm going to try to not drive myself crazy with it, as, to a certain point, what happens post-release will be out of my hands. I can't control review, buzz, etc. I can only turn in the best book I can. That said, I do feel lucky that my editor and agent are very enthusiastic about my work, that they don't run screaming from the phone when I talk about writing "different" or genre books and short stories. But if, after *The Little Sleep*, it turns out that Paul Tremblay can never work in that town again, well, I'll just pick another name. Like Nicholas M. Amatas. That would work, I think.

[Update: The Little Sleep *was acclaimed following its publication in March 2009 and follow-up* No Sleep Till Wonderland *was released in early 2010. Unfortunately, the economy collapsed in late 2008 and people were spending their money on ammunition and canned goods rather than books. Will Tremblay earn out his advances and sell more novels to Holt or another large publisher? Writing these words in the autumn of 2010, these questions remain unanswered.*

Paul Tremblay did return to the small press to co-edit the anthologies Phantom *(in which I have a short story) and* Creature! *for Prime Books. His short story collection* In the Mean Time *was published by ChiZine Publications in October 2010. A lesson—even if you make it to the majors, never forget the indies. And they won't make you change your name to fool bookstore computers like the majors will. Nicholas M. Amatas indeed!]*

[For some reason, I have become known as an opponent of self-publishing. Nothing can be further from the truth. I am a big fan of self-published material. In the 1990s, I loved reading zines. One of my favorite books of the first half of the 2000s was Stranger Things Happen *by Kelly Link, essentially self-published by Small Beer Press, which Link co-owns with husband Gavin Grant. What I am against is people being ripped off by self-publishing firms, and people who have written entirely ordinary commercial fictions acting as though they are rebels for eschewing commercial publication. Check out the appendix for "Attack of the Living Slush Pile" to see what the POD industry is like.*

With the rise of the Kindle and other ereaders, even those faux rebels might have something going for them. The Kindle has changed things, and the ebook market will continue to grow and lead to more opportunities for writers, even if the Kindle itself falls to the iPad or another competitor, which I think it will. Ultimately, we'll be reading ebooks off our smartphones or some other device we already have, rather than paying for a separate book-reading device. With Steig Larsson's series selling over one million copies in ebook form, the ebook has arrived, no matter what sort of screen we're looking at.]

Why Bother?

SELF-PUBLICATION USED TO BE A SUCKER BET 100 PERCENT of the time. Without distribution, one's self-published book simply gathered dust in one's garage. No reputable reviewer would touch a self-published book anyway. Vanity publishers stepped in with expansive claims of the benefits of paying for publication—Walt Whitman did it, as did Mark Twain, and besides, vanity publishers some-times run ads in *The New York Times Review of Books*, so that has to be good, right? Nope, vanity publishing was just like self-publishing, but with a sucker surcharge for the vanity publisher's profit.

Then came print on demand (POD), and the price of producing a book crashed. Tens of self-publishing compa-nies emerged, offering turnkey services for would-be writers. The best of these firms were straightforward in their advertising, and made no expansive promises about what POD publication meant. The other 99 percent of these companies made ridiculous claims. iUniverse, at one point heavily associated with Barnes & Noble, hinted that its titles would be carried in B&Ns all over the country. And a vanishingly small fraction of them were—in the Writing/Publishing section. Some POD outfits, such as PublishAmerica, basically pretended to be advance-paying "traditional publishers," despite accepting virtually every-thing submitted and paying all of a dollar (a literal dollar bill, in a frame) in advance.

POD and self-publishing have made significant inroads since then. Plenty of commercial publishers use a version of POD to keep certain backlist titles in print without racking up inventory fees, and a number of originally self-published titles have been reissued by commercial publishers. In some arenas, such as modern fiction written by black authors, there is no stigma at all to self-publica-tion; it was simply necessary, as New York spent decades ignoring the black market for transparently racist reasons. Only when black authors were able to move tens of thou-sands of copies of their books through networks of black bookstores, book clubs, handselling, and street vendors, did New York even understand that black people liked to read. Now, of course, most publishers have an "urban fiction" line and recruit heavily from the ranks of the self-published in that genre and demographic. (This shows what a raw deal self-publishing is—the self-publishing success story is almost by definition doing so well with one's homebrew book that it gets reissued by a New York publisher. You know you've made it big in self-publication when you don't need to do it anymore.)

And now we have ebooks. Of course, we've had ebooks for more than a decade. In the late 1990s, I remember the Gemstar Rocket reader making waves and projections that ebooks would be 10 percent of the market by 2005. It's 2010 as of this writing and ebooks are still not 10 percent of the market. But the 2007 launch of Amazon's Kindle did change the game. The great problem with ebooks is that ebook readers represented a several hundred dollar surcharge, but with Kindle, people finally decided that the surcharge was worth paying. And with the Kindle and its competitors (SONY's e-reader, Barnes & Noble's Nook, Apple's iPad, and various smartphones and PDAs of all sorts) taking off, and so, too, is self-publishing via these readers.

As a random author working in his or her underwear doesn't have to pay for New York real estate or cover design or health insurance, self-published ebooks can finally compete with commercially published material on a very important level: price. It's not unusual to find new writers putting their books up on Kindle, et al., for three bucks a pop, when the commercially published titles cost $10 or more. Suddenly, the "risk" attendant in picking up a book by an unknown quantity has diminished. Three bucks is what some city slickers spend on a single fancy cupcake, and ebooks generally don't have return policies, so three bucks is three bucks, and the majority of that money goes right to the author.

A number of midlist authors who retained the electronic rights to their books have had great success with Kindle.

Lee Goldberg has sold thousands of copies of his novel *The Walk* on Kindle, and made far more with his home-brew electronic edition than he did with the book's original publication in 2003. But, as he pointed out on his blog in 2010, "I have no doubt the big reason my out-of-print [titles] are doing as well as they are is because they are riding on the large readership of my *Monk* and *Diagnosis Murder* books." J. A. Konrath is another convert to the Kindle cause, and has even signed an exclusive contract with Amazon for his next book, but Konrath, too, had a built-in audience thanks to his commercially published thrillers and, more importantly, thanks to his blog posts on the subject of publishing. Konrath has an audience of readers, and also an audience of writers and aspiring writers who love his pro-Kindle rants and buy his inexpensive ebooks to support the cause. If you already have an audience from your commercial books and have retained the electronic rights to your backlist, you can make a killing with cheap Kindle releases. Well, for now. Once everyone starts doing it and there are tens of thousands of writers with three buck ebooks and a blog-shaped soapbox on which to stand and sell to the masses, who knows what the audience will do.

Starve Better is primarily concerned with the publication of short subjects, but the new ebook environment is even amenable to short stories. Short story collections these days are either small press affairs, or the indulgence of a prominent novelist, or the loss leader for a hotshot from one of the top MFA programs (and is usually tied to a future novel publication), But ebooks now lower that barrier just as they lower the barriers to novel publication. Anyone with a few stories can throw them up on Smashwords and make a few bucks. This is true of writers that have a substantial backlist of published short work, and also true of writers with nothing but a bunch of rejection letters and a stomach full of smoldering resentment.

So, after all that, why bother? Why sweat through the years of rejection letters, the paltry payments and tiny audiences of the magazines, the nigh-impossible task of breaking into anthologies, and all the rest when you can just write, upload, and watch the money roll in? Well, there are reasons.

The first is the most obvious: you're almost certainly an utter unknown, and even if very competitively priced, if nobody knows you, your ebook collection isn't going to sell more than a few dozen copies.

Selling a few dozen copies may sound okay, but can actually be harmful, thanks to the second reason—the short story, as it is an uncommercial form, exists primarily in a reputational economy. That is, as nobody makes a lot of money publishing short stories, payment comes in prestige. If you're a nobody and decide to inflict your otherwise unpublishable stories on the world in Kindle form, your prestige payment will be zero, at best. More likely, it'll be negative and you'll be seen as an untalented tyro impatient for the fame and fortune that some few people are making in the new ebook environment. And that brings us to the third reason:

You're probably a terrible writer. Being published on Kindle won't make you any less terrible. Getting a few fan letters from terrible *readers* won't make you any less terrible either. Nor will getting a few small checks.

If you're not a terrible writer, you should be publishing your short work in the magazines and anthologies. Really, *not terrible* actually is sufficient these days. Let them build your reputation—that's what magazines and anthologies are good at. Let them pay you, too. They're . . . not so good at that, but most short fiction venues of any reputation will pay more or less well for the marketplace, or at least more or less on time. We'll likely see an ereader-exclusive magazine sooner rather than later, and those new magazines will be well worth submitting to. Even the venerable *Asimov's Science Fiction Magazine* picked up something on the order of 4,000 additional subscribers via Kindle when it finally released its electronic version. This uptick, in the face of more than a decade of declining circulation, suggests that short fiction may have a home on ereaders. You just don't need to build your *own* home on the Kindle to get that audience.

The Book of Life

Despite my first love being the short story, and despite the relative success I've had with stories, I've only published about seventy—not including reprints—in over ten years of writing for publication. Even had I managed to sell them all to slick magazines that paid $1,000 or more, I wouldn't have made a living. This section will discuss other forms of freelance writing, with an emphasis on writing nonfiction for publication. Even the second and third-tier nonfiction consumer magazines pay far better than most venues for fiction. For fiction, a rate of twenty-five cents a word is stellar, and nearly unheard of. For nonfiction, it's a tiny bit low and easily attainable. One dollar a word is not unreasonable, so long as one avoids the absolute bottom of the barrel of blogging-for-hire, search engine optimization essay nonsense, and other sorts of work best left for semi-literates.

All that said, a number of these pieces, including the first, come from the fanzine *Flytrap*, for which I wrote a column named "Life Among the Obliterati" for the princely sum of $10 a pop. Why did I do it? My friends Tim Pratt and Heather Shaw ran the magazine, and I liked helping them out. However, even friends should pay something, and I always got my ten bucks promptly.

[Here's some advice I've taken in principle, if not necessarily in practice. I've written all sorts of nonfiction, from scholarly material to business journalism to "true" ghost stories, but have never managed to get any technical writing gigs, nor have I published in any trade journals. I've never even written a software manual.

Many successful writers can and have taken on these invisible jobs. Neal Pollack wrote brochure copy for Weight Watchers, and John Scalzi wrote a significant amount of corporate material even as his career as a science fiction novelist took off. A faculty member at the MFA program where I now teach even ghostwrote the autobiography of a porn star! Like the truth, the work is out there.

Since writing this piece, I moved away from and then back to California. I had health insurance only since 2008, when I got my first-ever full-time job, editing science fiction at VIZ Media's Haikasoru imprint. In the interim, I made sure to live in places with progressive politicians and local health clinics—Brattleboro, Vermont, Somerville, Massachusetts. That and some supplementary insurance from Western Connecticut State University, where I was enrolled as a student in its low-residency MFA program, kept me alive until I finally secured real health insurance.]

Makin' a Living

I WAS RECENTLY INVITED BY A BUNCH OF UNIVERSITY OF California, Berkeley students to talk on the subject of making a living as a freelance writer. I say "bunch" rather than "class" or "club" because they weren't either; I was expected to talk to them out in a courtyard and, worst of all, for an honorarium of zero. (Speaking before a college class or club generally brings in at least a hundred bucks or so . . . before a bunch of kids? I wasn't even offered lunch.)

I didn't bother to call them back to say I wouldn't come; my silent refusal should be object lesson enough. I had work to do anyway. However, the question "How do you make a living as a freelance writer?" is worth answering, if only to disabuse the asker of the unspoken assumptions that accompany the question.

First, let me make it clear: it is actually very easy to make a living as a freelance writer. I'm sure you've all heard the nonsense about how there are only a very few full-time writers out there, and that everyone else has to stitch together an income with a day job, teaching, or a generous spouse, etc. This answer is as wrong as it is common. It is true that only a very few writers do nothing but write; it is not true that they must have another job. Writers choose to have other jobs rather than live humbly. This brings us to the first hidden assumption involved in the question: writing isn't a job, it is a middle-class profession that should earn the practitioner both petit-bourgeois status and a comfortable income.

A significant fraction of writers who have a day job or a side gig as a teacher could live on their writing; they just don't want to, as it would mean a smaller house, a less pleasant neighborhood, fewer vacations, or less (perhaps even no) health insurance. That's an entirely valid choice, of course. Nobody gets any artiste points for eating beans and living in a garret. But wanting to live comfortably is not the same as being unable to live on one's writing.

I was asked, in the voicemail invitation, if I could explain the secret of getting affordable health insurance. Even if I had decided to do a free college talk, I suspect that the little Berkeleyites would have been shocked by my answer:

I don't have any health insurance. If I get sick enough to go to a doctor, I go to a walk-in clinic that charges $50 per visit and supplies prescription drugs out of the sample cases left by pharmaceutical company sales reps. If I end up in a persistent vegetative state with nothing but a feeding tube between me and Hell, well, the plug will be pulled within a few weeks. This is what happens to the uninsured.

There's no shame in not having any health insurance; I just can't afford any. Neither can millions of working people in this country, thanks to the bizarre agglomeration of private medicine, public insurance, and awkwardly regulated managed care regimes that most other developed nations were too smart to develop. And it's not as though the ranks of the uninsured and underinsured are filled just with bums like me. Ever been to a Wal-Mart? Like their low, low prices? You're paying for it another way. Wages are often between $7.50 and $8.50 an hour, and corporate healthcare utterly inadequate. One study "found that [in Georgia] 10,261 of the 166,000 participants in the PeachCare program, which provides healthcare coverage for youngsters in low-income uninsured families, were children of Wal-Mart employees. This was more than 10 times the number for any other employer." You subsidize public insurance for the poor so that Wal-Mart doesn't have to, and they pass the savings *and* the . . . uh, expenditure, on to you.

The difference is that while the U.S. as a nation seems to be callous enough to just shrug off the 40 million residents without any health insurance, nobody interested in a writing career would dare take a step toward fulfilling their dream if every little ah-choo wasn't accompanied by a brace of doctors. People who work in Wal-Mart (or McDonalds, or as career temps, or in the home) . . . well, they're apparently not even considered human enough to be allowed dreams.

Another major assumption in the question is that our middle-class writer will only write what he or she likes. Interested in writing for a market that pays two or three bucks a word and has almost no slush pile? Of course you are! I'd recommend checking out sample issues of *Trenchless Technology*, *Industrial Hygiene News*, and *Pit & Quarry*. Heavy industry not your thing? Why not get a gig writing speeches for your local state assemblyman, or copy for websites? Whenever I've suggested any of these possibilities to an eager aspirant, I've heard something along the lines of "But . . . that's boring!"

Sure is. Showing you where to find the toilet paper shelf at Wal-Mart at 3:00 a.m. on the morning of Thanksgiving is pretty boring too. But Wal-Mart (and fixing cars, and filling out insurance forms, and answering phones, and mining coal) are jobs. Writing is, to the curious questioner, an identity, a rarified identity worthy only of a certain class of people. The ultimate goal of a would-be writer isn't to write as a job, but to not have a job at all.

In most essays of this sort, we would now dust off various writing-related aphorisms: the money doesn't matter; if you don't have to write, don't write; be sure you have something to say. But this essay is different, so here is an actual, real-life piece of advice for those who want to write and make a living, however humble it may be, doing it: get the fuck out of the café with your little laptop.

Cafés are for dilettantes and people with day jobs. If you want to write for a living, as opposed to simply writing to perform an identity for coffee baristas and bus boys, you're going to need to learn to write at home, with screaming kids and household chores to be done (I've never been so neat and tidy as I am now as a full-time writer) and the ever-present television with its many siren songs. Writing for a living involves deadlines, and making deadlines without a manager breathing down your neck involves the discipline and mental focus to work in an imperfect environment. You'll be working when you're ill (no insurance, remember) and when it's 3:00 a.m. on the morning of Thanksgiving (after you pick up some toilet paper) just like every other working stiff in the U.S. Plus, given your likely income, you have better things to spend your money on than a seven-dollar brownie.

And there is one final reason why you shouldn't work in cafés: when I'm between assignments or taking a break, I like to go to a café and grab a little something. The last thing I want to see during my leisure time is someone trying to do my job. Just leave it home. I don't sit next to you at the movies and fix cars, do I?

["Makin' A Living" was published in May 2005, so I believe I beat John Scalzi to the punch when complaining about people who write in cafés. Also, in February 2007, I received this letter from a reader who was himself an aspiring science fiction writer:]

Hi Nick,

Just wanted to say thanks for an article you wrote in *Flytrap #4*. The one where you say something along the lines of "Anyone who says they can't make a living as a writer simply hasn't lowered their standards enough." Probably not an exact quote, sorry.

Anyway, it was the 4th of July at around 4pm in the [hospital] and my second son was going to be born in about 6 hours. I was sitting on a bed next to my wife during a lull in her labor pains. She was taking a much needed nap and I needed something to distract myself, so of course, I picked up the latest issue of *Flytrap*. I read your article. And the damn thing has clung to my brain ever since. In fact, it transformed in my brain as something of an inspiration. At the time, I was working in a warehouse, schlepping boxes while trying to get my fiction writer career off the ground. We were barely making ends meet with one kid and I didn't have a clue how we were going to make it work with two. But the problem was, other than writing, I have no marketable skills. Fast forward to now: as a direct result of that article, I'm a tech writer. Money's still tight, but not dire. And while it ain't exactly rewarding to write software manuals, it's better than working a warehouse. And every now and then, I think it actually informs my fiction writing.

I'm on a kick to thank people when they give me something (whether they intend to or not). So, thanks, Nick. You rock.

[See, it works.]

[During the great economic crisis of 2008–2009, I was in an odd position. I'd landed a very good job in publishing and could stop freelancing full-time. Indeed, I was even able to hire freelancers and recommend them for hire. What amazed me, though, was how little people knew about how to freelance outside of the field in which they'd already had some success. The fiction writers had no idea how to query nonfiction periodicals, and no idea how to find the sort of magazines they could write for, despite magazines being pretty prominently displayed in bookstores, on newsstands, and in virtually every other public arena. Even worse—a few friends arbitrarily decided that nonfiction magazines were "unprofessional" because they didn't deal with submissions in the same way penny-a-word fanzines do. Oy.]

How to Find Freelance Writing Work

LOOK FOR IT.

In 2005, for the Prattshaw project *Flytrap*, I wrote an essay about freelance writing and suggested that if you could not make a living as a freelancer it is because your standards were too high, both for what counted as writing and what counted as a living. A couple of years later, a new science fiction writer (he'd debuted in *Baen's Universe*) wrote me a letter of thanks. He happened to be reading the little zine in a hospital hallway while on the other side of the wall his wife was giving birth. At that moment, he decided to get together a few pieces of writing he'd completed in the hope of getting out of the job he had in a warehouse. He wrote to say that he credited my article with his new gig writing computer software manuals, which meant more money for his family. *[See "Makin' A Living," above.]*

This essay will be a little version of that. This isn't about making a living as a freelance writer, which is more difficult right now as ad buys are drying up and content migrating online in some poorly modeled ways, but about getting some money. This is also aimed at people in science fiction, who thanks to the raft of "writer-friendly" submission guidelines and close community ties between periodicals and would-be writers, have been reduced as a labor pool to a bunch of mewling infants unable to bathe themselves without triple-checking LiveJournal and begging advice from their Clarion teachers and Twittering about how hard everything is.

So, look for it. What you are looking for, specifically, are opportunities in nonfiction, as there are a lot more of those, and they pay better.

One looks for freelance writing opportunities by looking at actually existing magazines on newsstands and actually existing electronic magazines here on the WWW. You are not looking for "market lists," which are rife with obsolete information, and you are not looking for submission guidelines, which many magazines do not provide.

Note: you can also find the occasional gig via Craigslist. Do not write for start-ups who have yet to have a first issue. Do not send in complete articles. (They just steal them.) Do not bother with SEO nonsense. It's rare to find anything good on CL, but it's such a low-energy search that you may as well do it. Most recently, I found *H+* via Craigslist and have made $500+ for writing fewer than 2,000 words across two articles for them.

You are looking for magazines that you might like to write for, the articles in these magazines, and then on to the masthead for either a) a submissions address, b) the contact information for the editor of the department you wish to write for, or, barring that, the c) contact information for the managing editor. Once you have your magazines, you do not want to write to the top of the masthead (editor-in-chief, publisher, senior editor,) or to the "copy editor" (who is not in charge of buying copy, but in charge of making sure copy isn't embarrassing) or anyone else like that.

What you are looking for, for the most part, are second and third-tier magazines. This is because they often depend on freelance work and because nonfiction works differently than fiction.

When writing fiction for publication, especially science fiction and fantasy, one is told to a) finish a story and then b) send it to the magazines that pay the most and are most widely read first.

In nonfiction, this is not the done thing. You start from nearly the bottom to get a little money (and even tiny magazines generally pay better than the short fiction "markets" people are used to) and to generate clips. In nonfiction, few people buy articles. They assign articles based on ideas. The evidence that you are capable of writing an article is an actually existing and published article you have written. In nonfiction, one works one's way up. When I was very serious about nonfiction, I turned $50 gigs from Disinfo.com into $500 gigs for the *Village Voice* into $1,500–3,000 gigs for *Artbyte, Silicon Alley Reporter*, and *Razor*. Note that I never made it into the top tier of slicks, mainly because that would have required a bit more party-going and shoeleather journalism than I felt like doing. But $1,000 for a few email Q&As and maybe a phone call suited me just fine.

Also note that the three slicks I wrote for regularly are now defunct. That's fine. There's always a lot of churn in the marketplace. All that lives must pass from life. This is God's way. To kill you.

There are two types of magazines in the marketplace, incidentally.

The type that always need new material.

The type that run the same fifty stories over and over again over the course of say, eighteen months.

To generate ideas for the first type of magazine, think of things are either in the news or soon will be. Then forget your first two ideas and develop the third. For the second type of magazine, just think about what isn't in the issue you're looking at, but should be.

Another note: under no circumstances are you to suggest a "follow-up" to an existing article.

Then you write your query letter, which begins not with who you are or anything like that, but with the succinct articulation of your idea. The hook. (This hook will later become your nut paragraph in the piece itself.) In the second graf of the query, you write a tiny bit about why you are qualified. Then you offer clips.

Yet another note: You aren't writing anything but query letters until you get an assignment. Almost nobody wants to see finished articles. (Indeed, most writers are very dubious of the few magazines that want finished articles, as they may end up working for free.)

In the old days, by the way, queries were even done by phone. Think of your hook in this way. You've got a busy stranger, not necessarily well-inclined toward you, on the phone. What do you say to keep her on the phone? Well, here's what you don't say:

"I'm sorry for taking up your time, but . . . ."

"Are you taking queries?"

"I'm Smedley Vanblunderchump and I've published a lot of science fiction short stories in magazines you never heard of and I want to set your readers straight on the LIE of global warming, because I think *Sierra Magazine* needs to run articles on the other side of the debate, aka THE TRUTH . . . ."

Here's an example of a query letter (yet another other note: I didn't attach clips to the bottom of this one because it was my second piece for *The Smart Set*):

2009 is the 200th anniversary of Edgar Allan Poe, arguably the most famed and influential writer in American history. Not only does his work entirely limn the culture, he created no fewer than two genres of popular fiction—mystery and modern horror—virtually by himself. His poetry is still widely read, his personal life and discontents inform the clichés of the starving writer in his garret AND the mad genius, and it's virtually impossible for someone to graduate from an American high school without having read Poe.

Not bad for someone whose themes represent a near-total amorality, a distaste for Enlightenment values, and a complete separation from American society. Unlike other early American writers, Poe's material cannot even be used in schools to teach about Puritanism or slavery or any of that other social science stuff that has colonized the Language Arts departments. Poe has nearly been defanged by grade school teachers, but he is too darkly vibrant to be put down for long. Poe, in his rejection of all things "American," IS needed by America. He is the antidote to cultural complacency.

I propose a think piece on Poe from a reader's point of view. I'm a horror writer myself, so will make some mention of his connection to the popular culture, but am primarily interested in digging up the Poe that rests partially occulted under a big pile of fourth grade school assignments and such. Why are we teaching kids how to read with stories of uncomplicated revenge and slaughter, and teaching how appreciate critical reasoning by playing with the absurd. (It was an orangutan!)

About 2500 words'll do me. What do you think?

So, as you can see: there's a news hook (200th birthday), applicability (everyone is familiar with Poe), a twist that makes the idea new (reclaiming Poe from schoolteachers), and a bit of why I am the one to write the piece (I write horror). If it's a bit more casual than you expected, that's only because I'd already worked with the editor before. (And I'm awesome.)

Then you are good to go. This went well enough that after "Poe at 200" came out and I collected my $400 for half an afternoon's work, the gang over at *The New Humanist* asked for a Poe article—like the one they'd read but aimed for their audience—and offered £150 for one quarter of an afternoon's work.

Not famous. Not a big deal. Perhaps not even magazines you'd ever heard of. But they pay well, quickly, and are eager enough for work that they may solicit based on a published clip. This is what you want when you want money for freelance writing.

Which magazines should you query? Well, in the second and third tier there is no reason not to query all of them. Send the same query to a bunch of places, with tweaks necessary for slightly different audiences. It's fine. Everyone knows that queries are non-exclusive. Indeed, everyone knows that ideas are non-exclusive. Your contract may say that you should not publish a similar story to the one you sold for thirty or ninety days. The second magazine may demand fresh quotes from various sources (just keep a few good quotes to yourself so you won't need to re-interview anyone), but it's not a big deal.

The late, great D. G. K. Goldberg was a travel writer, and she once told me of the Smartest Writer in the World. He, too, was a travel writer, but he never left the house.

He lived near Orlando and wrote the same broad strokes article once a month, every month, for his entire career. He did service journalism about Disney World and the various other attractions in the area.

"Going to Disney for Christmas?"

"Five Best Hotels for Your Disney Trip."

"Plan Your Summer Trip to Disney!"

"Five Can't-Miss Disney Attractions!"

Who bought these articles? Well, parenting magazines, family magazines, travel magazines, regional magazines (all regions), religious magazines, airline magazines, community newspapers, and daily newspapers.

Did the editor of Magazine B ever see this guy's story in Magazine A? Surely. Hell, that's probably how the Smartest Writer in the World got the gig at Magazine B.

Moving on.

Once you get a nibble on a query, write the article *on time* and to the specifications agreed upon. Once the piece is published, *that is your clip.* So, if we're talking a paper magazine, get copies and save some, then scan the article or at least get some decent photocopies for faxing. With this clip, aim upward to the next tier of magazines.

If it's online, just use the URL. (It might be smart to print out a few copies though, as websites go away sometimes.)

And soon, the world will be yours.

An Aside: Counting the Keystrokes

I find many of the comments regarding the financial aspects of writing short fiction hilarious, primarily thanks to the implicit notion that there is a better per-hour or per-word (hell, why not per-keystroke) return to be had in writing novels instead.

This is especially funny today because every Wednesday, the book-sale measuring service Bookscan updates, and I have access to Bookscan. I like to, once a week, check out how the books of various friends—some of whom have landed "good deals," others of whom have recently embarked on ambitious tours and promotional efforts—and count up the books sold for them this week.

Assuming a 100,000 word novel and an advance of $5,000–$30,000, and the number of revisions for novels both pre- and post-sale and the very low sales most of them generate, and given the fact that low sales can limit the opportunity to sell subsequent books (short stories don't have this downside), well, you know what? Here are some numbers.

These, in random order, are the number of books sold this week by various writers whose blogs I read with some regularity. These are all books from major publishers that came out in 2009 and represent a variety of genres (fantasy, mystery, western, mainstream). Some of these numbers are from multiple award nominees and winners, a couple are from people who have been prominent for decades. I'll not attach any identifying material to these numbers, but they are the ones I check every week:

trade paper originals: 38, 34, 5, 39
mass market (some original, some reprinted from TP): 50, 24, 724*, 117, 44, 249, 39

Of course, many people sell many more books per week. And many people sell short stories for four-digit sums to slicks and have them optioned for motion picture

---

*724 sounds pretty good, except the book has already been out for three weeks as a mass market original (with a traditionally short lifespan on the shelf), and this number represents a 14 percent drop from last week, which was a 22 percent drop from the week prior.

adaptations, or use the publications to secure lucrative public speaking and teaching engagements as well. But if you're looking to maximize your earnings per keystroke as a tyro, pooh-poohing short fiction to instead write novels is pretty silly given the few chances one gets with novels, the amount of post-acquisition revision that goes into novels (more keystrokes), and the sales your basic novel is going to garner after only a few weeks or a couple of months on the shelves.

[Do you know what people will spend a lot of money on during an extended economic crisis? How-to books about writing! You know what else? Resumes, cover letters, and other such nonsense freelancers certainly don't need.]

And Now on to Freelance Writing Work, Part II: Writing For Non-Publication

HOW DO YOU GET WRITING WORK THAT DOESN'T INVOLVE publication?

Be the writer in your social circle.

If you spend a lot of time hanging out with other writers, going to your little writer's group, and not talking to anyone who isn't fascinated with writing, writing, writing, you can stop reading now. Sucker.

Remember that our goal here is fast money for writing, not a living doing technical, business, or commercial writing, which is great and pays a lot (I have friends who bill $85–$125 an hour for pamphlets and such) because it just takes a long time to break in. And speaking of suckers, people have degrees in this dumb crap sometimes these days. Though, like a lot of computing gigs, business writing is one of the highly paid jobs that one can snag without a degree.

Fast money requires a start near the bottom rung: local, local, local. Cover and business letters, business plans and web copy for local businesses, privately published books for local institutions and individuals. You find these by basically being "the writer" on your block.

In 1997 I moved to Jersey City, years before gentrification took hold. (Hell, twelve years later gas stations are still being held up by men wielding potatoes.) My landlord figured out that I was a writer in a perfectly Holmesian way: I never left the house, I was always a couple days late with the rent, and I was typing all the time. This guy, Azad, was very smart and a hustler besides. He always had something cooking with real estate, with the social club of which he was president. I also knew this other guy named Sam, who did a little of everything for people. He was a notary public and had a fax machine and Internet-ready computer, etc. in a time and place where many people didn't have instant access to these things.

I became their scribe. Five bucks a page for things like writing a business letter, or a letter to immigration services for one of their friends, or a cover letter, or a flyer for a party they were having. And their friends started wanting to open businesses too: barber shops and bodegas and such. So, letters to the government, filling out forms, and business plans ($15 a page for those). English-language skills were trade skills. They didn't have them, I did. They might have spent hours agonizing over the writing of a formal business letter and ended up with a semi-comical paragraph of hypercorrect British English (these guys were mostly Indian and Pakistani) and aural copy errors ("strubroorn" for stubborn was one that took me a while to figure out) and even the poor cats needed a letter and had $5.

Of course, five bucks is nothing. Absolutely nothing. But it's five bucks more than you get for writing Blog Post #8264319812 about how one can't find a job, innit? What takes these clients hours and days would likely take you a few minutes. And while it can be difficult to gain the trust of immigrant populations, especially if you're some Aryan god stupid enough to end up poor even with all the advantages of your peeled-potato face and a surname that sounds like you just spit out some food, well, remember that there are a lot of whites who are so stupid they don't even read my journal! You're a little brighter than they are, you ugly caveman. They need cover letters and resumes free of typos as well. My fave was someone who came to me with a first draft: the objective was "a job in fund-raiding" instead of "fund-raising." Truth in advertising doesn't pay. Then there was the woman who had as one of her skills "proofeating" . . . .

You'll also benefit from the ridiculous advice of career coaches: when people lose their jobs they often try to start a business and get money from the local bank. This might even be a good idea in some recessions, but not one in which the recession is caused by the banks losing all their money on financial instruments made up of 200 side bets per poorly constructed ranch home. But career coaches never change their tune and dreams die hard. So your little pals and homely aunties and whatnot are going to need their business plans done and copy for their stupid Etsy stores and a little pamphlet to hand out and all that rot. Don't believe me? Here's some copy from an Etsy shop that will remain unidentified:

> You will receive this with a description of ways to wear. Just two easy steps. No zips No closers . . . You put your head in to two holes! Curious? . . .

See, there's a would-be clothing designer who needed a friend to write some copy for a few extra bucks.

Being "the writer" in your circle is kind of like being the person into films in your circle. If making videos is your hobby, you'll inevitably be asked to videotape a wedding, for example. The same with writing. Just be sure to hold out for some dough. Your church will need a newsletter and perhaps some tracts. Someone with a real job might throw some corporate work your way. Then there's private or institutional publication as detailed here. (I ended up making a cool grand doing a little work for a firm like this. My qualifications were that I was "a writer" and the person doing the hiring was a friend's roommate.) Local volunteer fire departments, old biddy societies and their plans for a spiral-bound cookbook, stores that have been around for a hundred years, these institutions are ripe for the picking—they have websites. One of their members might stumble across lulu.com and decide to do a privately published book.

And remember to bill. There's no political movement or local historical event or ethnic group so precious that you must work for it for free.

You'll note that the plan here presupposes some involvement in the social world as opposed to, say, the social networking world that is already text-based and thus generally doesn't need a scribe caste. If you're crazy and alone and do nothing but play World of Warcraft all day on the computer and don't even talk to your relations, much less friends or associates, well then you need more help than I, or Facebook, can give.

[As most people interested in this book will be coming from the world of science fiction, fantasy, and horror, I'll spend some time on writing nonfiction for various fiction venues. Note that most of the markets for fiction pay the same for their nonfiction—between five and ten cents a word. However, one must remember that twenty-five cents to a dollar a word isn't unreasonable. There are good reasons to write for genre magazines, though: you can meet some of your favorite authors, get your name in front of editors, and occasionally get free books or DVDs.]

Work Your Way Up

IN THE WORLD OF FICTION, ONE SHOULD SUBMIT FROM THE TOP down. That is, after one writes a short story, one should send it off to the best magazine for it—best being defined as the magazine (or rare open anthology) with the greatest reputation, the largest circulation, and the highest rate of pay. Of course, we're talking within the field. Your hard science fiction opus of libertarian engineers conquering the asteroid belt for a mining concern isn't going to find much play in *The New Yorker*. *Analog*, however, would work just fine. After collecting that near-inevitable rejection slip, you move on to the second-best magazine or anthology. With nonfiction, however, things are different.

Nonfiction is based on the clip—publications in small magazines, or local ones, are attached to query letters to larger magazines. Remember that nonfiction assignments come based on query letters, not completed assignments, but editors hand out assignments not simply based on the ideas pitched to them, but on their estimation of the writer's ability. And those estimations are largely informed by clips. So, how do you get clips? You start from the bottom and work your way up.

As I mentioned in another piece, I got my start writing blurbs for a website for $50 a pop, then parlayed that into bigger paydays with bigger magazines and websites. You can do the same. One substantial marketplace for nonfiction comes from the magazines with an emphasis on fiction— fiction magazines run reviews of books, interviews with writers and editors, and literary essays of various sorts. They don't pay very well, but they can be that first rung on the ladder. Here are some tips on what to do, and what not to do.

Reviews: reviews generally come in two types—capsules, and review essays. Capsule reviews are those obnoxious little summaries with perhaps a single sentence of evaluation. The essays are longer. My strongest recommendation is to write these reviews less like a fan and more like a discerning critic. There is an enormous amount of what I call "fannish handicapping" in the reviews of small magazines—is book X science fiction or is it *really* fantasy? Is its cover "trying" to be mainstream? Is it horror disguised as a thriller? This sort of taxonomical dithering is of absolutely no interest to anyone who edits or, for that matter, reads, the more prominent magazines.

I'd also avoid being "cute" (e.g., using words like "frak"), extensive first-person asides about how you just don't like books about werewolves, and the use of the language of fanfiction—referring to characters as "Mary Sues," for example. Remember, you're not just writing a review for the audience that might actually know or care what a Mary Sue is, but for every editor you hope to impress in the near future.

What you should do when writing a review is this— find some essential element of the book that either makes it a successful read or an unsuccessful one, and communicate that essence to the reader. When I reviewed China Mieville's book *Kraken*, for example, what I noticed was:

> The real star of *Kraken* is its comically lugubrious narration. Near the end we're told, for example, "the kraken would give them this transmutation, this squid pro quo, by the contingencies of worship, toxin, and faith." The book is a love letter to a certain gonzo vision of dark fantasy— the results of crazy die rolls in homebrew role-playing games, bloody black-ink doodles on the margins of labor history textbooks, an apocalypse that ends the world neither in fire nor in floods, but in post-modern post-everything snickering. There are iPod playlists that give more accurate predictions than Tarot decks, and the narrative's many asides and infodumps are more interesting than any ol' squid that isn't even in half the book anyway.

The review is chatty and light, but not simply a series of in-jokes or knowing nods, and it actually deals primarily with the text—in this case, the narrative voice Mieville uses, complete with a brief but telling example. (Long quotes from a text both eat into word count and annoy many readers, who just skim over them anyway.) The ultimate secret to reviewing well is being a discerning reader, and that only comes from practice and the ability to read through a book even if it isn't immediately engaging or your sort of thing. Just keep reading with an eye toward structure and effect.

Interviews: interviews also fall into two types: the personality profile (an article with quotes and flavor text) and the Q&A. Both are great in that subject does a lot of the writing for you with the answers to your questions. There are some discontents, however, mostly with the Q&A.

Email is both boon and bane when it comes to Q&A assignments. Email means no more misquoting, no more transcribing from tape, no more long phone calls or missed connections. It also means the end of the follow-up question. It is just too easy—for both interviewers and subjects— to accept a single list of questions and fill in the answers. There is something to this technique; Samuel Delany prizes what he calls "the silent interview," but Delany also takes the questions he's asked and uses each as a jumping off point for an extended essay. Any sort of interview technique will work if the subject is a cooperative genius.

For the rest of us, interview by email can lead to some tedious reading. An explosive answer like, "I write because it's the only thing that keeps me from killing people. That's not hyperbole, I really mean it. I LIVE FOR BLOOD!" is followed up with, "So what are you working on now?" (Certainly not killing people!) Even worse is the interviewer who uses the same exact questions each time—though it is mostly bloggers who do such things. And those bloggers aren't impressing anyone.

The solution is easy, if you can get the subject to participate. Either a "live" online interview using a chat program that keeps logs, or one email at a time. Anything from IRC to GChat will do—for "off line" commentary, work out some method with the subject, such as putting background questions and answers or requests for clarification in parentheses, for easy editing out. Sending one email at a time can be a challenge, but makes for excellent interviews, as a "real" conversation can be generated, and with the additional advantage of giving the subject a lot of time to formulate an interesting answer to each question.

Then there are essays. We don't have the space to run a text-based workshop on writing creative nonfiction, but we do have the space for another list of pitfalls. Essays are, as the word implies, *attempts*. A proper essay isn't a five-paragraph term paper of the sort we as a society foolishly train first-year college students to write. It's an attempt, through the very act of writing, to come to some kind of conclusion. An essay requires a bit of a veering off from the classic elements of oration: exordium, narratio, etc., to find a new truth, or to fail to do so. Too strict a structure, especially if the words "In conclusion" (or any variation thereof) appear in your final paragraph, is a recipe for tedium.

As with reviews, avoid the sort of fannish material and counterpunching—essays about some other essay or blog post or guest of honor speech at a convention—common to blog posts. A little shoeleather journalism can go a long way, though essays don't require the same level of first-hand research or sourcing that feature reportage does. Most of all, though, avoid making pronouncements; a real personal essay, or even a literary one, will hint at some vulnerability, some awareness that you're not objectively the hero of your own life. Check out "The Term Paper Artist" later in this volume for an example of what I hope is a successful attempt to hint at vulnerability.

Finally, don't spend your life hustling after these low-level SF/fantasy nonfiction markets. The goal is to develop clips to bring to local magazines, trade journals, and even national venues and websites. While one shouldn't make a habit of turning down work, the early nonfiction material must be produced with an eye toward climbing the ladder. Soon, you'll find yourself being solicited for work rather than hustling for it all the time.

[This piece was an expression of frustration over the inability of some of my friends to use their skills to make some extra money. Ego is so often the obstacle—by being afraid to fail, they failed by saying "no" when they should have said "yes." Specifically when they should have said "yes" to me and all the money I had to spend on freelancers.

One additional note on solicitations—to begin with, at least, you'll be solicited at less than what you make on a query or through submissions. That is, if your fiction is beginning to find its way into professional magazines or anthologies, you'll first be solicited by fanzines or semi-professional venues. If an editor for a nonfiction magazine requests a pitch or offers an assignment, it'll likely pay less than the periodical in which the editor first saw your material. This is fine to start. Though you'll get a bit less money here and there, more publications and new relation-ships with editors is a good thing. Eventually, though, you'll be able to set a minimum rate for your work, and there's no need at that point to say "yes" to every solicitation you receive . . . unless they can meet your price. For your first several solicitations, take what you can get, and remember, don't work for free.]

Taking the Next Step:
This is How You Freelance

IF YOU START DOING A FEW THINGS HERE AND THERE, eventually you'll reach a point. The point will take the form of a person who will treat you differently than others have treated you. This person, at this point, will ask you to do something. You'll be used to asking others if you might do something for them, or even just doing something—say, writing a short story—and asking others if they'd like to license it from you.

But this is different: at the point we are discussing, someone will ask you first. You'll be solicited to perform some service or produce some product. This is the correct way to respond to a solicitation, if you are at the point of your first (or first dozen or so) solicitations.

Step One: Say yes.

Step Two: Ask how much the pay is.

Step Three: Ask for specific details on the project.

These steps must be performed in this order. You start by saying "Yes." "Yes I will write X/send you audio file Y/ produce drawing Z," etc. Then you ask how much you'll be paid. If the payment is not acceptable, then your yes may become a no. By saying yes, first, however, you have baited the hook. You are more likely to find the money offered rising to meet your price if you agree first and then complain about the low wage or fee. If you ask about the fee first, you have no room to move.

You also do not want to ask about details first, as details are just that—details. What you are actually willing to and able to do is best discussed after acceptance and pay have already been hammered out a bit. That way you can argue for more money or less responsibility based on the details. If you ask for details first, and worse, make unpleasant noises about them, the person soliciting you may become less enthusiastic about working with you . . . and you haven't even said yes yet so there is no informal psycho-social agreement that would compel him or her to keep talking to you.

Under no circumstances should you say any of the following—all of which I have heard in my own role as a commissioning editor—when you have reached the point of being solicited:

1. I'm not good at that.

2. I don't know very much about that.

3. Well, it's under Creative Commons/you can just link to it from my own webpage.

4. Why shouldn't I just do it myself and keep all the money?

5. I'm really busy.

If you're not good at something, you now have the chance to get good. If you know nothing, get to a damn library. If someone just wanted to link to something, they would have. Don't be a yutz—if you were capable of doing something yourself and positioning it or distributing it in a way that would create money for you to "keep," you likely would have done it in the first place. Nobody who wants to freelance and who just got his or her first solicitation is too busy.

If you follow the conversational pattern I've laid out above and actually manage to do the work on time (of utmost importance) and very well (of secondary importance—complete, mediocre, and on time is better than perfect and late), you will start receiving more solicitations and become a good freelancer. Good enough to start turning down solicitations after the first couple dozen or so. If you do not follow the conversational pattern I've laid out above, but instead make one of the rhetorical errors

I've discussed, you are telling the person at this crucial point one thing and one thing only:

"No thanks, I'd rather die in the gutter."

[Fun fact: I was rejected as a writer for Demand Studios, one of the leading content mills, in 2010. A number of my friends make a few bucks—emphasis on few—with the site, so I hope the following doesn't come off as sour grapes. It did make one of my friends feel better about her own career with the site when she heard that my voice and style weren't suitable for projects such as 500-word essays on backyard shed-building. The ability to write to order is a valuable skill, even if content mills don't pay for it hardly at all.]

A Note on Content Mills:

or,

A SUPERSONIC TSUNAMI IS

GOING TO KILL US ALL!!!

THE WEB NEEDS CONTENT TO SURVIVE, AND CONTENT, UNTIL recently, didn't come cheap. Blogs, user-generated content on bulletin boards, Wikipedia—that stuff's all free or near-free. But there are opportunities for paid publication on the web outside the realm of online magazines. Websites need copy, and to generate that copy a new form of business, the content mill, has emerged.

The first content mills were launched in the 1990s. Epinions, which is still extant under very different terms, paid a dime a hit for short articles about any ol' thing one might want to write about. It was originally positioned as a consumer-generated alternative to *Consumer Reports,* and tons of wannabe writers hit the site hard. For a few months there, some busy beavers who reviewed basically everything they owned or experienced and then spammed the web and USENET made a few bucks from the site. Back in 2000, during the height of the dot-com boom, *San Francisco Chronicle's* Carrie Kirby reported making $73 from putting up some old notes on a trip to Asia, and reported that Brian Koller, an amateur film reviewer, made over $500 after writing and publishing three hundred movie reviews on the sites. As time went on and epinions—like many sites of the era—realized they had no way to monetize the copy, the payment schedule tightened up. Soon people were being paid only for the hits from other epinions members, and today most active users earn nothing.

Modern content mills have solved the problem of paying for content by positioning themselves as middlemen, so that some other bunch of suckers can make the payouts. Demand Studios, one of the most famous and well-regarded of the content mills, provides most of the content for eHow.com for example. Writers who sign up for Demand Studios and make it past the initial screening period can expect to make $15 for short articles such as "Tai Chi for Plantar Fasciitis," to name the one and only article I wrote via Demand Studios. Shorter pieces, some only two or three sentences long, can earn three bucks. Demand Studios always has work, though the work can be nonsensical—"How can I Learn Wolf Style Kung-fu?" was one question I saw on a list of assignments when looking into Demand Studios. Too bad there is no such thing as wolf style kung-fu.

There are other content mills as well—Suite101 is a site of long standing and back in its early years it wasn't unusual for dedicated freelance journalists to place their articles on the site after initial publication in a paying magazine. As with many other parts of web 1.0, Suite101 has evolved into a content mill. Today, the site pays $3.90 per 1,000 page views, and some of their authors can make a four-digit monthly income from writing hundreds of articles. Of course, many more writers make almost nothing from the site—posting there is purely speculative, financially speaking. Naturally, a content mill will, like a weight-loss plan or Amway, hype their top performers, not their average performers. Three bucks ninety is actually pretty good for mill; competitor Associated Content only pays $1.50 for every thousand views, though that site also has Demand Studio-style up-front payment for some of its assigned content for third parties.

Helium.com does the normal mill sort of thing of allowing anyone to post anything with no fact-checking or notion of accuracy, but also has a Marketplace section where their better writers can develop articles and use Helium as an agent of sorts—the site sells the pieces and pockets a commission. This supposedly makes more money than the ad-driven content, but I do remember seeing an article on Helium about the BP oil spill of 2010 that claimed that a 500-foot-high *supersonic tsunami* could erupt from an undersea methane gas bubble and destroy much of the American south dozens of times on Facebook, Twitter, and other blogs. That gasbag probably made a lot of dough, and without knowing the first thing about science.

Many writers complain that content mills are an online proof of the validity of Gresham's Law. Aw, I'm teasing you—most writers don't know what Gresham's Law is; they just complain that the mills pay pennies where they once could have made dollars. Gresham's Law is basically: "bad money drives out good." In the old days when coins were worth something based on metals from which they were made (e.g., copper or gold), the "good" coins made of gold would be hoarded, while "bad" coins that had been debased or that were only valuable because the government said they were, would be traded. And so it is the same with content—debased content drives out good content on the web, thanks to content mills.

And the content is often bad. After a decade of free-lancing for some of the better magazines and alternative newspapers in the country, I was rejected from Demand Studios by its editors for not using enough "action words" in my articles. One of the assignments I claimed was on training in the use of swords and knives. I wrote about various schools of fencing, both Asian and Western, and what to look for in a teacher, some safety recommendations and cautions, the whole bit. However, the piece was labeled *how to* and apparently that meant that I needed to begin the article not with an overview but with exciting verbs. Had I started the article with "Step one: *grip* the hilt of the sword with your right hand, and then *swing* it around," that would have been acceptable to the editors. Two action verbs, right in the first sentence! Now that's writing, in the Internet age. I'm sure someone took up that assignment and did a good job with it, and that it was worth every penny of the fifteen bucks he or she was paid. And if someone ends up lopping off his own head following the directions of a writer whose qualifications were to shout "Me first!" when seeing the open assignment, well, *caveat emptor.*

Also, content mills are a rip-off. The top earner for Suite101 in 2009, according to CBS's Bnet.com, Lena Gott, makes a couple of grand a month, thanks to her 200+ articles. Two hundred articles even in a second-tier magazine that pays a quarter a word would pay out at around $80,000. If the Suite101 payouts continue at the same level for three years, if her position is not usurped by competitors either within or outside the site, and if she doesn't keel over from exhaustion, then she'll break even. Or she could have written maybe a tenth as much for real magazines and made her $24,000 a year.

Breaking into the magazine market is easier said than done, but so, too, is making anything close to a living wage in content mills. What is utterly average for magazine writers is the peak of the profession in the mills, and mill writing is generally inadequate for getting bigger paydays from better venues, for developing a reputation as a writer of quality, or even for writing about what you like consistently. The problem is that with the ubiquity of the Internet and the inability of the average reader to tell the difference between bad content (e.g., *supersonic tsunami*) and good, those well-paying magazines are suffering and the content mills are booming.

Mills are good for something—Demand Studios and other mills that pay *up front* are good for the utterly desperate. A few acquaintances of mine, including one who was once named a "Writer on the Verge" by the *Village Voice,* swear by their favorite mills. The payouts are a little bit less than even academic ghostwriting (see "The Term Paper Artist" in the appendix) but they're consistent and the work is easy once you shut off your brain and forget completely about quality. And forget about growth. Writing for little magazines can lead to assignments from big magazines—content mills have zero growth potential. It doesn't matter if you're an expert or a novice, if you've written a million articles or two, if you've developed a following elsewhere or just landed on this planet from Mars, you're just another comma monkey to the faceless mill editors.

If you need money now and have no illusions about doing anything other than sweating out a bunch of articles over the weekend just to get a quick fifty bucks on your PayPal debit card, then yes, turn to a content mill. But don't let the mill turn into a full-time job. Like their physical namesakes that sucked the life out of endless numbers of American workers, today's content mills do not have your interest at heart, and nothing you can learn from working in one will equip you to get out of the backwater 'burgs of the Internet and on to the big city of real paying gigs. And today's millwork is already being offshored, just as the textile mills were themselves closed down and relocated overseas a generation ago. There are plenty of competent English speakers in India and other developing countries where U.S. dollars are expensive relative to the local currency. The competition for those fifteen-dollar gigs is going to be very keen very soon. If you don't have the skills to compete for real assignments from quality magazines, and you have nothing to offer that a writer in the developing world can't do as well as you can already, you may find yourself moving from scraping the bottom of the barrel to living under one.

Appendix

[I wrote "Attack of the Living Slush Pile" for the Village Voice way back in 2001. A number of the players have changed—iUniverse and XLibris have changed owners and business models a few times now—but the central problem with POD technology and self-publication hasn't. Even with the Kindle, the main issue is that everyone thinks they can write thanks to their third-grade educations. Once you know how to write a sentence, after all, what is writing a novel but writing 20,000 of the little buggers in a row?

I was amused at some of the nasty letters I received when this piece was published—one accused me of being a shill for "corporate publishing," as if these POD presses weren't being heavily funded by major publishers, bookstore chains, and investment banks. Now, of course, the big money has moved on to ebooks, but the POD vanities are still kicking. As I write these words, Xlibris is offering a deal: sign up by September 15th and you'll get expedited service so your book will be ready in time for Christmas. The website features a kindly old man reading a book to a young girl in front of a fireplace. I wonder if he is reading her a thriller about abortion survivals and ratmen . . . .]

Attack of the Living Slush Pile

THE VANITY PRESS IS AN ANCIENT IDEA, BORN JUST ONE DAY after the first rejection slip. Under the old model, vanity presses would print a few thousand copies for an exorbitant price, even if the elite of the New York publishing industry considered the book unmarketable.

These days, the author of a science fiction novel like *Alien Armageddon* can buy his way out of the slush pile. For a three-digit fee, he can get his work published through a new print-on-demand outfit like Xlibris or iUniverse, loosing on the world such classic bits as "Having surveyed the whole planetary system, the sphere narrowed quickly on the curious emitter of universal interference. And there it was, sailing knavishly through the blackness of eternity."

Print-on-demand houses solicit clients online, then use the latest technology to crank out only enough books to meet existing orders—a run so small the book would sink in the mass market. Sounds good, but the problem is that a lot of these books should sink, because they're poorly written or because their audience is limited to the far-right fringe.

Print-on-demand writers rake in whatever they can through selling their books—often by hand and on their lonesome. Not only doesn't Xlibris depend on author sales, the company probably wouldn't survive if it did. As of November [2000], its best seller had moved only "somewhere between 1,000 and 2,000 units," says CEO John Feldcamp. Half of all sales go to the "pocket markets" surrounding the author—friends, family, a few bulk sales if the author can arrange a signing or a reading, the occasional classroom placement.

While there are a number of very good Xlibris books available, especially those that were once part of a standard royalty publisher's list, an examination of randomly chosen Xlibris fiction titles reveals a catalog full of clichéd plots and terrible-to-middling writing, not to mention downright bizarre notions of the world.

One title, David L. Buhlman's *Final Warning*, billed as "an adventure story about a bleak near future that may be more likely than most would care to admit," imagines life after a takeover by the pagan-feminist New World Way. "In order to control population growth, people are put to death at age sixty, abortions are forced, and the sickness of pedophilia is legalized and encouraged. But with boys only, not girls. Girls are protected because they are identified with the goddess Gaia, the religious myth that undergirds the New World Way. The mainline Christian denominations are forced to insinuate the Gaian rituals into all religious ceremonies, and religious leaders who would not cooperate are imprisoned." The novel also features cloned ratmen who probably aren't Christian either.

Nineteen Eighty-Four it ain't, but Feldcamp insists such a title has a market. "Do we have an obligation to say that that author can't reach that market?" he says. "No, we're not a publisher. Traditional publishing works great for publishers, but not for authors. . . . It excludes 95 percent of the books that are written." Feldcamp claims sales will increase as the publishing industry shifts, but the bottom 95 percent of all books written will not be driving any changes in publishing if nobody is buying them.

And publishing hasn't changed enough yet. Xlibris, in January [2001], hiked prices on its services, laid off employees, canceled the long-running e-mail newsletter Inkspot, and delayed plans for expansion into the European market.

iUniverse has its share of winners (or is that wieners?) as well. *And Then You Die*, by John Robert Jorrisen, begins with a homeless woman finding six fetuses in a rubbish bin outside an abortion clinic cleverly nicknamed "The Butcher Shop," and as the book tells it, one of these aborted fetuses "was moving!" The bag lady quickly adopts the embryo as her own and walks off with it in her shopping cart. What market does this book have? Pro-lifers who insist that abortion is murder, but might consider that sometimes it is merely assault? Would-be adoptive parents looking for a cheap alternative?

The nonfiction is often little better. iUniverse presents *America Under Siege*, by Robert W. Pelton, a book that claims "untold numbers of hostile foreign troops as well as thousands of Russian tanks, trucks and other military vehicles are being brought into our country," a notion made famous by the right-wing militia movement and only true when those "untold numbers" are very, very low. Xlibris offers Charles Munn's self-help book, *Becoming the Thinker*, which promises that you "will be flooded with the serene knowledge of your inner power as you project your desires and mold the future." Wow!

These books are sold alongside more reasonable titles like iUniverse's *Campaign and Party Finance in North America and Western Europe*, an academic book that may have a very small audience, but which does deserve to be in print. Indeed, it probably deserves better than the iUniverse treatment.

The publisher made a splash following an investment by Barnes & Noble, America's leading book chain, two years ago. Posters and brochures at B&N promised that you, too, could become a published author. B&N even carried some iUniverse titles, albeit in the Writing and Publishing section of their bookstores, where wannabe writers hang out.

iUniverse's profile was raised by its association with B&N, but the iUniverse authors were left out in the cold. Harry Youtt, the chief grievance officer for the Los Angeles local of the National Writers Union, started following up on complaints made by iUniverse authors and found that many clients felt abandoned by the company. Books were frequently printed and delivered late, and iUniverse officials offered little in the way of explanation. An informal survey of B&N stores by Youtt found "most stores indicated that they only stock iUniverse titles if they are part of a 'special promotion.' Several stores stated that they thought they carried some iUniverse titles but had no way of identifying any. Several indicated they had never heard of iUniverse."

There were other problems as well, including the accidental elimination of 400 iUniverse titles from its online bookstore and database. There was even talk of a class-action suit against the company last year.

In October, iUniverse received another influx of cash, this one from Warburg Pincus Inc., an investment bank. iUniverse immediately laid off many of its columnists and community leaders and de-emphasized its vanity operation to concentrate on business-to-business projects. iUniverse is using its technology to get into ebooks, having made deals with IDG Books Worldwide (of the "Fill in the Blank for Dummies" series) and the distributor Publishers Group West. The happy faces of iUniverse authors are long gone from the website's lead page, and the iUniverse bookstore is [in 2001] buried under a couple of layers of links.

Prodded by groups like the Authors Guild and the Harlem Writers Guild, iUniverse is bringing some important books back into print. Mike Levine, the former DEA agent turned government critic, brought his *New York Times* bestseller, *Deep Cover*, back thanks to iUniverse and the Authors Guild's program, BackinPrint.com. Unlike the vanity customers, Levine didn't have to pay a cent to get iUniverse to reissue his book. BackinPrint.com has also negotiated with the Shakespeare & Co. bookstores to carry these particular iUniverse titles. Bringing works back is inherently less risky than accepting work from people whose only skill may be filling out a check for $99, and these works have built-in audiences, whereas most wannabes have only their elderly relatives and anti-ratmen activists.

Random House Ventures, LLC, the investment subsidiary of Random House, Inc., has invested heavily in Xlibris, but not for the rights to the vanity firm's massive list of titles. "Random House is not interested in much in the short term," Feldcamp says, but the investors do "think hard about the future." And in the future, it is unlikely that the vanity press will be any more profitable than it is right now.

Print-on-demand and ebooks will change the publishing industry, but the importance of an editorial filtering system to spare customers from bad writing is clear. Book editors and their fiefdoms, institutional paralysis and all, will survive even a takeover by pagan-feminists and homeless fetuses driving Russian tanks ahead of an army of ratmen. They've already faced worse, in the mountains of unreadable slush filling their offices.

[Here is a piece that was widely linked to, and widely misinterpreted. Here's the shorter version: to be a great writer one needs to die and then be declared great. To set yourself up for that you need to write something that cannot be denied by mining your inner self.

The most common misinterpretation simply ignored the actual method of becoming great—dying and being declared great by others. Folks pointed to writers who haven't yet been declared great, or pointed to obstacles in being declared great (e.g., being a woman writer). All true, but not really relevant. In the end, one cannot decide to become a great writer, they can only decide to become the sort of writer who might one day be declared great.

Others took issue with the notion of "greatness" itself, because it was "patriarchal" or "elitist." This would shock many a great writer were they alive, since many of them were considered losers and failures by their contemporaries. A few people floated the idea of "excellence" as opposed to greatness, but excellent writers are a dime a dozen anyway. There's no need to be a great writer, but if you'd like to be one, you may as well give it a shot.]

How to Be a Great Writer

A CRITIQUE SERVICE CLIENT, AFTER GETTING MY REMARKS ON a 9,000-word excerpt of a novel, asked:

> Do you think I have potential to be a great writer? The thing is, whenever I ask this of other people, the answer is usually "well, everybody has the potential . . . " which I always thought was bull. I don't want to merely be publishable

(although that would be beyond what I am right now). I don't want to just be good. I want to be great.

Stephen King was rather blunt when he said that only some people have the right stuff. I didn't like it when I first read *On Writing*. But he was perfectly right.

Do you think I have it?

Stephen King's perceptions are warped by his peculiar place in the world. He is a rare bird—a great writer who is not a good writer, and whose influence on writers who are neither is so profound that it is hard to pick out his personal greatness from the tsunami of crap he sparked by that long-ago cannonballing into a small sump in somewhere in southern Maine.

Your friends are actually closer to right, but they cannot articulate what is actually going on because they are unaccustomed to thinking about greatness. We live in a Starbuckized "democracy," after all. We satsifice and market that as excellence; we don't excel. Everyone does have the potential to be great, but that level of potential varies widely, and this variation is based on exogenous factors. In music, having perfect pitch as a toddler is handy, and if you have perfect pitch in the right place and time you can end up being the world's greatest violinist. In another place and time, say Long Island in the middle-1980s, you can end up being Debbie Gibson (who was indeed a toddler with perfect pitch). Over course, 100 years from now the world's greatest violinist may be considered a racket-making poof and Debbie Gibson could be the subject of innumerable theses and popular v-books and smellovision documentaries, but that just shows that "greatness" continues to be influenced by exogenous factors posthumously.

The issue of greatness in what you are trying to do—popular fiction in the early 21st century—is a matter of mental training. Ronald Sukenick, in a different context, spelled out what one must do in the form of this warning: "If you don't use your imagination, somebody else is going to use it for you." (There are those exogenous factors again.) The trick is that one of the most popular ideas in other people's imaginations is that greatness is a matter of some inner spark, a pilot light that is either on or off. No, it is always off to start, but may be turned on through dedicated practice.

The practice of which I am speaking is not the usual shit of reading widely and writing daily and revising with vigor—that's how one becomes a good writer, not a great one (and it is best to be both, of course). Instead, one needs a certain mental discipline. One cannot just run around thunkin' up gunks; if you want to lick thirty tigers today you need to be in a tiger-lickin' frame of mind. That discipline is oriented toward a single thing:

You have to stop caring whether you live or die.

This is not just apathy about life, but a more active denial of the social world. You have to get comfortable with the idea of walking around without skin, with not caring at all whether or not your parents ever speak to you again, with not stopping after your lovers all leave in teary huff after teary huff, whether your book sells two thousand copies or two million, whether or not everyone knows exactly what imagery you masturbate to. This doesn't mean merely being confessional, but simply ready. If your imagination—your imagination—suggests that the best solution to some problem you have is the insertion of your right arm into a wood chipper, you must eliminate the social, personal, and autonomic buffers that would keep you from doing just that.

This will not make you a great writer—it will turn on that pilot light, though. Only accidents of history make people great writers.

Getting to this point is a lot of hard work, and often people attempt to achieve this state through drugs and alcohol (Burroughs, even King) or through privation (Hamsun, Fante) or through various antinomian praxes (lots of people—great writers tend to be awful kooks, even when kookiness might involve never quitting one's job as a CPA and marrying the first person who smiles at you). There's no one way to do it, and most ways fail for most people. Like *gongfu*, you have to eat bitter before you can taste sweet, though you may well die before ever tasting sweet.

The hardest part is actually to figure out how you are wired sufficiently well to engage in the practice in the first place. You'll need to try many things and fail many times.

The goal of the practice is to negate the negation—to eliminate the use of other people's imaginations instead of your own. You must negate and negate and negate until there is nothing left but you, your right hand, and that wood chipper. Do you think it is clever and responsible to find "balance" in your life by keeping a day job and writing every other weekend? You should cultivate a loathing for yourself, for such advice, and for the pathetic circumstances of existence—bills and kids and private property, that makes that advice seem so sound. Do you think "real artists" run around from lover to lover, living off the fat of the land and friendly patrons one might meet in midnight cafes? Embrace the reality that you are a hopeless poseur playacting the neuroses of a couple prominent writers and zillion awful pigs from the last century. All that has come before is worthless, except for those few people you realize were using their own imaginations and not the mass imagination, and their work.

King is a useful example here. He is a great writer because he lets it all hang out. His hopes and sentiments, his awful bitterness, those wounds that never heal and those scars across his body and psyche which he cannot help but count and re-count more frequently than he counts his millions, his essential kindness (which informs the avuncular tone of his work—King is like a cruel dentist who hates his own cruelty even while he reminds you of what a masochist you are for being in his chair), his outrageous inferiority complex vis-a-vis contemporary American realism and its publishing infrastructure, it's all fucking there on the page. He doesn't care whether or not he lives or dies, not in the sense we are discussing now, and he wouldn't care even if he wasn't the world's most popular writer. Under another set of circumstances, S. King would still be the barstool intellectual and substitute teacher who writes a novel every six months and throws it out; he just married someone who didn't dig the manuscripts out of the trash. He would write this stuff for free, as he himself has said.

If King leaves it all hanging out there, which is what makes him great, his innumerable clones simply also leave it all hanging out there, but what they leave hanging for public display is King's stuff. They are using Stephen King's imagination, not their own. Most of them have no idea that they even have an imagination that was not sold to them by King's publishers and the movie studios. That is why not one of them is great. They have spent some effort on being good and publishable writers—they write every day, learn their Strunk and White by heart (aside: Strunk and White is NOT concerned with grammar, but rather with style; never confuse the two), are sure to change the ribbons on their typewriters, and meet their deadlines. They may as well be working in a concentration camp. Did the ovens meet their quotas for "processing" today? All scum, all the time. After giving birth to this generation of scum, it is no surprise that King concludes that greatness is inborn rather than an artifact of practice and circumstance. To say otherwise would be like cursing one's own children.

Of course, King isn't a very good writer. He loathes the sentence, doesn't understand the paragraph, cannot write anyone not of his generation with any level of fidelity, is overly enamored with eye dialect, obviously phones it in when tired or bored, cannot edit himself (which is what makes him great!), and, like Ray Bradbury, cannot overcome his early childhood fascination with cheap tricks. Like Bradbury, however, he does get that they are tricks, and presents them as such. And that's why he is great.

So, do you really want to be a great writer? Magnum Opus No. 1 has to be the rewriting of your own personality so that it is proof against the mass personality of the common imagination.

[If you're reading this book and have already made it to the appendices, you surely don't need a Masters of Fine Arts degree in Creative Writing. Partially because you already know more than most grads—well, unless you've flipped to this page in the bookstore without reading all the previous chapters. Partially because plenty of writers have made a go of it without school. And partially because readers of Starve Better *are most likely interested in genre fiction, which the faculty of most MFA programs have little experience with. And yet, more genre writers are looking at MFA programs— one can spend a couple of years being taken seriously as a writer, and potentially get a teaching job with the credential of a terminal degree. I got one myself, at Western Connecticut State University's low-residency program. I teach there now as well, as the semi-official "science fiction" guy. Come see me if you want a genre-friendly educational experience. You already own the assigned textbook. Except for you bookstore page-flippers . . . .*

These next two pieces, published in The Writer *and* The Writer's Chronicle *respectively, cover the pros and cons of MFA programs and of the issue of genre in the academe. The material about workshopping is applicable to Clarion, Odyssey, and even local writers' groups as well. Plus, if you wish to make fun of MFA programs and those literary poseurs, you'll have some ammunition now.]*

How to Get the Most Out of Your MFA Program

MY MFA EXPERIENCE WAS UNUSUAL, TO SAY THE LEAST. AT the end of my first semester, for example, I shared with my fiction instructor two things: a rejection letter from a literary journal, and a sneak peek of a starred review in *Publishers Weekly* for my second novel. I'd been a free-lance writer for over a decade when I went back to school, but I learned a lot, both from the many great writers (both students and faculty), and from a recurring sense of déjà vu. The struggles of my fellow students reminded me of a whole bunch of stuff I had learned back when I was matriculated in the School of Hard Knocks. No MFA program will make you into a writer; you have to start thinking like a writer from your first day a class. Here's what you should do.

DO Read All You Can

This may sound like silly advice, and yet, lots of students don't read. Occasionally I heard, "I don't read because I don't want to be influenced by others." Every writer is influenced by the work of others, and this is a good thing. Literature, journalism, new forms such as creative nonfiction, it is all a series of conversations writers have with one another across generations.

"Well," one of the guys I was hanging out with asked me, "what about the first writers ever? They didn't read; they had nothing to read." They also weren't very good. The surviving classics of the ancient world came from the oral tradition—the first scribes wrote down the good stuff and left the junk to vanish. Trying to write without reading is like trying to swim without ever visiting the water. But what should you read?

- Read what you want to write: You need to keep up with the field. Your science fiction adventure is going to be instantly obsolete if the last space opera you read was an old Star Trek novelization. You may think poetry reached its height with the Shakespearean sonnet, but editors will wonder why your stuff rhymes, and why it reads like kid's stuff.

- Read faculty publications: Forget celebrity; the best faculty mentors are the ones whose writing is simpatico with what you want to do. Find like minds by checking out your professors' books.

- Read everything else: Read the classics, even if they bore you. Check out experimental literature, even if it confuses you. And read a bunch of paperback novels from the supermarket, even if you think them beneath you. They all have something to teach.

And, of course, you need to read the assignments your fellow students hand in for your workshops, which brings me to my next tip . . .

DO Leave Your Ego at the Door

The writing workshop is designed to do many things. It keeps students writing on a schedule, teaches them how others read and misread creative work, and develops focus and critical ability. The success of a writing workshop depends on you, and your ability to have some distance from the work.

- Keep your mouth shut when your work is discussed: you won't be there to explain that some far-fetched incident in your story really happened, or what the bluebird symbolized in your poem, when it's being read by an editor, so it's futile to defend your work in class. Don't argue, don't complain. You can accept critiques or reject them, but do so in silence.

- Remember that you are not your story: you are not being critiqued, even if your piece is a memoir, or even if the work came from a deep and secret part of your soul. Your classmates are talking about words on a page, not your personality.
- You are not a psychology major: by the same token, you do not have a special insight into your classmates from reading their work. The student who hands in a story written from the point of view of a murderer isn't a killer waiting to strike. If something gets under your skin, you have probably encountered that rarest of workshop submissions: effective writing.

You are in your MFA program not just to read or to talk about writing, but to spend a couple of years actually writing. Keep in mind that writing isn't an end unto itself—you also want your work read. So, keep these two tips in mind:

DO Pursue Publication

I've met more than a few MFA graduates who had no idea how to submit their work for publication. Sometimes, professors even tell students to concentrate on their "art" and to leave the commerce for after graduation. I'll be blunt: they are wrong. Most writers, historically, learned through years of submitting and collecting rejection slips. Even the most rarified and exquisite piece of literature you've ever read went through the submission process, by definition. It had to be published to be read. So, to publish:

- Start at the top: submit your work to the most prestigious, most popular, and best-paying venues first. As the rejections roll in, work your way down. Yes, your stuff will get rejected by the *Paris Review* and Binky Urban, but all you'll have lost is stamps and time. If you get published, the rewards can be great, unless you settle for some obscure webzine or a photocopied journal nobody reads.
- Think ahead to your thesis: Novels are in greater demand than short story collections. A bundle of random stories, or a collection entitled Every Poem Since Eighth Grade, probably isn't going to set the publishing industry on fire. You have two or three years to write, so get to work early and write something you'll be able to publish.
- Don't publish yourself: you won't fool anyone who isn't easily fooled by using a self-publishing service or a new small press you just happen to own. Don't try to fool yourself either.

DO Meet People

"It's not what you know, it's who you know" is true, up to a point. Few people have cocktail party patter so smooth that they can talk themselves into a book deal, but making contacts is crucial. There are tons of ways to meet people:

- Start a blog and update it regularly: you don't want to publish your own fiction, poetry, or formal essays on your blog, but you'll find that it is a lot easier to meet publishing people online than nearly anywhere else. Use your blog as a soapbox, as a place for personal stories, and as an idea generator.

> Get involved in the big conversations going on in the
> literary blogosphere.

- Attend events, readings, and soirées: at the very least,
  you'll find that literary events are often a good way
  to get some free protein in the form of hors d'oeuvres.
  This is a crucial trick for starving writers.
- Write letters: famous authors are routinely badgered
  by kooks, but the not-so-famous are often very open
  to hearing from their readers. Don't ask for favors
  (like "Please read my work!") out of the blue, but
  strike up correspondences with some up-and-coming
  writers. You might be surprised what a casual email
  can lead to.

Now we should talk about a few of the things you
should not do if you want to get the most out of your MFA
experience.

DON'T find excuses to avoid revising: Your work will
probably generate mixed opinions. This is not the time
to throw up your hands and say, "Well, half the people
like it and half don't so I don't know what to do," as I
heard so often in my workshops. Not one of these confused
workshoppers actually listened to the people who recommended changes; they took the path of least resistance. Yes,
there will be credible opinions in your workshops, and
useless ones; your job is to be able to tell them apart and
act accordingly.

DON'T "obey": While revision is crucial, revising simply
to comply with instructor taste or, even worse, to make the
workshop happy, is ridiculous. Revision should have one
goal: making your piece the work you want it to be. You
cannot satisfy everyone and should not try to, even when
grades are at stake.

DON'T keep score: There's no way to "win" a workshop. There are plenty of workshop superstars who have never published a thing, and an enormous number of writers who did just fine without taking a single writing course. The only thing that matters is what's on the page, not what some famous faculty member said about you once, or how annoying the loudmouth next to you is.

DON'T "have experiences": Of course, you should live life, but don't jump out of an airplane or sleep with strangers or move to Tanzania just to have something to write about. If you have something to say, you'll learn to articulate it. If not, all the wacky adventures in the world won't make you more interesting. Remember, whatever doesn't kill you will only make you seem desperate.

DON'T think your degree means anything: An MFA degree and two bucks will get you a ride on the subway. A credential doesn't mean that you're a writer and it doesn't mean that agents and editors are dying to hear from you. It's the words that matter, not just three letters. Make every word count.

Aside—On the Down Low:

Most of the advice works for low-residency MFA programs as well as on-campus learning, but here are a few more tips for those writing from home:

- Learn to use your computer: many low-res programs use distance learning software and email. In my program we had a student show up in the "virtual classroom" halfway through the semester because she couldn't figure out how to log in. That's like spending weeks wandering around campus, looking for the right building.

- Teach: there are few low-res programs with teaching assistantships, but teaching experience is vital for an academic position. Hit the community colleges, continuing education programs, and adult and child literacy programs to get some experience.
- Make time: traditional MFA programs are a two-year break from life in which to write. Low-res programs are about finding spare moments to write while living. Set aside time every day to catch up on correspondence, read, and write. Time management skills will help you throughout your deadline-intensive writing career.

[The low-residency advice, though scant, is especially impor-
tant for genre writers, as the programs most open to genre
writing also tend to be low-residency programs, as we'll
see now with "Pulp Faction." With the work of Raymond
Carver and other "dirty" realists being eclipsed by the post-
modern fabulations of David Foster Wallace, Aimee Bender,
and other great contemporary writers, there is also a greater
tolerance for genre work in otherwise mainstream graduate
writing programs. Don't expect to get to Iowa on the strength
of your Heinleinian military SF opus, but sneaking in a ghost
or two is no longer to risk general humiliation in a writing
workshop.]

Pulp Faction: Teaching "Genre Fiction" in the Academy

IN 2006, SARAH LANGAN PUBLISHED HER FIRST NOVEL, A
supernatural thriller called *The Keeper*. It has all the hall-
marks of a classic horror novel: a New England setting,
bizarre family secrets, a town full of nightmares, and a
mass market paperback release. You can find *The Keeper* in
most any supermarket or drug store, in addition to every
major bookstore. If there's a difference between Langan's
book and any other horror novel published last year, it's
that the prose is elevated, a bit more "literary" than one
might expect. Maybe that shouldn't be a surprise; after all,
Langan received an MFA from Columbia University and
even workshopped the novel there. Or maybe we should
be surprised that Langan wrote a horror novel at all.

"In one workshop, my professor announced that I was
ruining a perfectly good book," Langan explains, "and had

the class vote, by a show of hands, on whether I should exculpate all supernatural elements." Indeed, all over the country, the occasional writer of fiction other than the realist or postmodernist material historically valorized by the academy has found herself stymied in trying to get an education. Haddayr Copley-Woods, whose fantasy and science fiction short stories have appeared in the online journal *Strange Horizons*, among other venues, got her MFA at the University of Minnesota, where she frightened her professors. "Professors feared I was committing cultural misappropriation by writing what they saw as magical realism—except, tellingly, a dual citizen Mexican-American adjunct who loved what I was doing."

As a teaching assistant at Minnesota, Copley-Woods allowed genre fiction in the undergraduate workshops she facilitated. "The kids from working-class backgrounds were thrilled that I would let them write fantasy and SF; the middle-class kids, by and large—except for some of my hard-core nerdy computer tech students—sniffed at it." She was instructed to warn her students that if they submitted genre work as part of their application to more advanced workshops the department offered, it "would guarantee that they wouldn't get in." Copley-Woods explained to one student that fantasy was disallowed because "so much of it is badly written," and one student fired back, slamming his fist against his desk as he said, "If it's all so badly written, wouldn't it make sense to teach us how to write it well!"

Now that student may well have a place to go. Over the past several years, a number of schools have launched low-residency MA and MFA programs that offer the opportunity to write and workshop commercial fiction. The granddaddy of them all is probably Seton Hill, a Catholic university in Greensburg, Pennsylvania. Seton Hill's MA program in Popular Fiction encapsulates SF and fantasy, mystery/thriller, romance, and writing for children and young adults. Michael Arnzen, horror novelist and associate professor in the English department, says that Seton Hill offers a focus on "marketing issues, trends in genres, business matters, etc. We bring publishers and agents to campus as guest speakers, in addition to recognizable 'name brand' writers." Popular culture is taken seriously, and not just as an object of study, but as something in which students and professors actively intervene through their fiction.

While Seton Hill is the only program that concentrates exclusively on genre fiction, several other programs allow for concentrations. Goddard College's low-res MFA has a track in speculative fiction, an umbrella term of art in popular fiction circles for science fiction, fantasy, and horror. Stonecoast at the University of Southern Maine also offers a complete popular fiction curriculum in the genres, alongside tracks in fiction, poetry, and creative nonfiction. The popular fiction track is market-oriented, as is Seton Hill's, according to faculty mentor and science fiction writer James Patrick Kelly. "I don't teach formula," he says, "but I do say 'this is how it's been done before'," to student writers who are engaging with science fictional ideas, sometimes for the first time. Between residencies, Kelly demands dozens of manuscript pages from his students and annotations of books on subjects as varied as time travel and deadly poisons. Graduate-level "intensity," says Kelly, is definitely a part of the Stonecoast experience.

Teaching genre fiction is different from the realist fiction that dominates most MFA programs. "I feel conflicted about saying this," Kelly says, "but it boils down to plot-driven versus character driven. You must have plot," for a successful genre piece, and "plot is part of character." Kelly's conflict is ironic: in the science fiction world, his own SF is sometimes castigated as "li-fi," a play on the term sci-fi that paints Kelly's work as too "literary" to be proper genre material.

In teaching SF, there's another aesthetic issue that emerges. SF has often been called "the literature of ideas," and simply planting a domestic drama or an action-adventure story in outer space will not do. SF is all about "ideas in play" and "big concepts" that psychological realism often keep in the background, according to Kelly, and much of the time in Stonecoast workshops is spent talking to students about the places "where their ideas don't add up."

The workshop and the basic elements of teaching fiction remain essential even in a genre context, however. Arnzen notes that "the basics elements of fiction matter more than anything else, and though every genre emphasizes them differently, every writer needs to master the basics. A text is a text; genre is more of a context." When the context is missing, that's when problems can emerge. Sarah Langan experienced this firsthand at Columbia. Undoubtedly one of the top MFA programs in the world, her workshop experience occasionally left her wanting. "When I handed in fiction that didn't quite click, the impulse of the workshop was always to remove the supernatural. It's the easy, obvious fix when you don't read genre, or know what how it's supposed to work," she says. "That kind of fix tends to homogenize." Copley-Woods had a similar experience with the failure of context in her workshops. Some of her professors "had it in their heads that SF is supposed to be bad . . . they froze in the face of my crappy stories," and were at a loss as to how to make them better.

"Crappy" genre fiction goes part of the way toward explaining why genre fiction hasn't been embraced by most writing programs, despite the demand for such training. It can also explain why low-residency programs are taking up the slack. Low-res writing programs are already the "junior partner" in most schools that have organized them, according to Kelly, so it is no surprise that they are the ones to take the risk of teaching genre. "The academe is slowly becoming reconciled to the fact that we're writing literature," Kelly says. Arnzen believes that a syncretism is on the horizon. "Mainstream popular fiction today is also committed (albeit unconsciously, I think) to the aesthetic of realism as much as those writers working in MFA programs," he says, and he credits the dominance of cinema in the contemporary imagination.

There is a counter-aesthetic on the bookstore shelves, though, one that further suggests that the non-realistic may have a place in graduate writing programs. Work by Murakami, Jonathan Lethem, and other writers demonstrate a mastery of the literary, the tropes of popular fiction, and the non-realistic. These are the writers the new generation of graduate students has spent the last decade reading. The commercial low-res programs may thus find an odd bedfellow in those MFA programs committed to experimental writing. Experimental writing often elides into genre fiction through the remixing of popular culture, the collapse of high culture into low, and the emphasis on ideas over the psychology of the middle-class subject. Brian Evenson is the chairman of Brown University's MFA program, and publishes regularly with publishers dedicated to experimental and academic fiction like FC2 and Coffee House Press. He's also published, under the name B.K. Evenson, straightforward genre fare—an *Alien* tie-in novel. "At Brown, we're really interested in literature that falls outside of the boundaries of realism or that complicates realism in some way or other."

Evenson is also the winner of an International Horror Guild award for his FC2 collection *The Wavering Knife*. He was "a little surprised" by the win. In 2007 his novel *The Open Curtain*, which combines Evenson's interest in

---

Mormonism's secret bloody history with aspects of both surrealism and the thriller, was nominated for the Mystery Writers Association's Edgar Award for Best Paperback Original Novel.

Genre fiction is sometimes "more dynamic than what traditionally gets labeled 'literary.' Plus, there are great readers," says Evenson. "I don't know if it's really an elision of the commercial and the literary so much as just an indication that categories of fiction that are sometimes dismissed as genre are actually quite a bit more complicated than we originally thought." Evenson also sees that realism's stranglehold on the academy's imagination is loosening, with "the *New Yorker* publishing writers like George Saunders and with traditionally literary magazines like *Conjunctions* [for which Evenson works] publishing work that straddles the line between literature and popular fiction." He also points to the ascension of pulp writer H. P. Lovecraft into the literary canon—Lovecraft's stories have been collected by both the Library of America and Penguin's venerable Classics line—and even "the acknowledgement of graphic novels as a legitimate art form," as further signs of a new conception of what is literature.

Then there is also the question of what is marketable. The genre-themed tracks and writing programs are focused much more getting their students published commercially than are many traditional programs. It's not unusual for a student to collect her MFA, and after two years of intensive study have no idea how to even format a manuscript, or where to submit it for publication. Indeed, even at Stonecoast, the "literary fiction" students aren't getting the same emphasis on publication. Kelly recalls a residency wherein he "got into it, a little bit" with one of the literary fiction students for whom genre was anathema. Finally, Kelly asked the student "if he had submitted anything. The student said 'No'," and then explained that he didn't know how to revise his stories, and was waiting to complete his MFA. Then he'd be able to rewrite, the student believed, and would learn how to submit his work. Among Kelly's own students, by way of contrast, some of them come into the program having already published short stories. Sandra McDonald, one of Kelly's students, has already sold a trilogy of science fiction novels to Tor. Her first novel, *The Outback Stars,* was released in May 2007. Seton Hill has its share of well-published alumni as well. Mary SanGiovanni's thesis novel, *The Hollower,* was acquired by Leisure Books as a paperback original and was published in September 2007. "In most MFA programs, students tend to produce theses that are either story collections or poetry collections. We focus on novel-length work, which has some of its own demands," Arnzen says. And some of those demands are resolutely commercial.

Evenson believes that the split between literary and genre fiction in graduate writing programs "has everything to do with when writing programs began to flower." Class may be another essential issue. Not only were graduate programs in writing emerging at a time when genre fiction was considered subliterary, they were emerging at a time when there were significant barriers to working class participation in such programs. The divide between literary and genre fiction can in part be laid at the feet of popular magazine marketing at the turn of the twentieth century. The "slicks," with their large middle-class audiences, were dedicated to realism, thanks to the influence of William Dean Howells and his followers. The "pulps," printed on cheap paper and sold to the newly literate urban working classes, concentrated on fiction that its audience could relate to. Working-class lives were transformed far more profoundly by industrial and social technology, the core element of science fiction. Urban areas seemed awash in crime, thus the mystery/detective story. Fantasies,

Westerns, and romances all harkened back to various mythic Golden Ages long since lost to urbanization and rationalization.

Today, as Copley-Woods noted in her experience, it is the "the kids from working class backgrounds" who want to write genre fiction, and increasingly these kids and adults are the ones attracted to low-residency programs. Arnzen has found the same at Seton Hill. "Low-residency programs appeal to working class students and economic pragmatists," he says. "They appeal to the students who want to fit learning into their own workdays or lifestyles. In fact, low-res programs almost always have to advertise this way, to make up for what they're losing from residency programs." Like science fiction itself, genre-themed MFAs may just be a glimpse into the future.

[Of course, maybe you don't want a graduate degree in writing, but you can still profit from the educational system. I made a fair amount of money from the dubious job of term paper artistry over the years, though these days term paper artistry is often "outsourced" to workers in India and other parts of the developing world. The old term paper system of brokers and contractors couldn't compete on price—especially not when brokers took $20 per page for themselves and paid their contractors only $10 or $15. Folks in business for themselves, whether in India or Indiana, can charge fifteen bucks a page and keep it all. Of course, they also have to take the risks involved in trying to collect money, find clients, and deal with customers who are almost by definition cheaters.

Leaving aside the moral issue of paper-writing—my position is essentially that higher education as a system is so saturated with corruption that nothing can make it worse anyway—this sort of scut work is still widely available. In the old days, the demand was for written pornography at short fiction and novel length. Then, papering. Now, Search Engine Optimization (SEO) copy for websites and working for content mills.

SEO and content mill work is a source of great concern among freelancers since it seems like real writing. After all, milled material is "published," and term papers are not. And the money is pathetic. Five and ten dollars for 300- to 400-word articles is pretty much what a writer will get at first, and the coop generated isn't useful as clips to get better gigs. After all, magazines can get interns to write 400-word blurbs. There's no need to hire a 400-word "expert," especially when the requirements for online copy—specifically Googlability—are so different from the requirements of standard nonfiction writing.

On the other hand, three 400-word essays can't take more than two hours, and that can be a quick thirty bucks all snug and nice in your PayPal account by the end of the day. Do

company press releases, and those "9/11 Was An Inside Job" bumper stickers. It's custom-made Cliff Notes. Virtually any subject, almost any length, all levels of education—indulgent parents even buy papers for children too young for credit cards of their own. You name it, I've done it. Perhaps unsurprisingly, the plurality of clients was business administration majors, but both elementary education majors and would-be social workers showed up aplenty. Even the assignments for what in my college days were the obvious gut courses crossed my desk. "Race in The Matrix" was a fashionable subject.

The term paper biz is managed by brokers who take financial risks by accepting credit card payments and psychological risks by actually talking to the clients. Most of the customers just aren't very bright. One of my brokers would even mark assignments with the code words DUMB CLIENT. That meant to use simple English; nothing's worse than a client calling back to ask a broker—most of whom had no particular academic training—what certain words in the paper meant. One time a client actually asked to talk to me personally and lamented that he just didn't "know a lot about Plah-toe." Distance learning meant that he'd never heard anyone say the name.

In broad strokes, there are three types of term paper clients. DUMB CLIENTS predominate. They should not be in college. They must buy model papers simply because they do not understand what a term paper is, much less anything going on in their assignments. I don't believe that most of them even handed the papers in as their own, as it would have been obvious that they didn't write them. Frequently I was asked to underline the thesis statement because locating it otherwise would have been too difficult. But that sort of thing was just average for the bottom of the barrel student-client. To really understand how low the standards are these days, we must lift up the barrel and see what squirms beneath. One time, I got an e-mail from the broker with some last-minute instructions for a term paper—"I told her that it is up to the writer whether or not he includes this because it was sent to me at the last minute. So if you can take a look at this, that is fine, if not I understand." The last-minute addition was to produce a section called "BODY OF PAPER" (capitals sic). I was also asked to underline this section so that the client could identify it. Of course, I underlined everything but the first and last paragraphs of the three-page paper.

The second type of client is the one-timer. A chemistry major trapped in a poetry class thanks to the vagaries of schedule and distribution requirements, or worse, the poet trapped in a chemistry class. These clients were generally lost and really did simply need a decent summary of their class readings—I once boiled the 1,000-page *New Testament Theology* by Donald Guthrie into a 30-page précis over the course of a weekend for a quick $600.

Others are stuck on their personal statements for college applications and turn to their parents, who then turn to a term paper mill. One mother unashamedly summarized her boy and his goals like so: "[My son] is a very kind hearted young man. One who will make a difference in whatever he does. Barely can go unnoticed because of his vivacious character, happiness, and joy in life. He is very much in tune with his fortune and often helps the less fortunate." The kid planned to be a pre-med major if accepted, but was applying to a competitive college as a Women's Studies major because Mother was "told the chances of him getting into [prominent college] under less desirable subjects (as opposed to Business) was better." Finally, she explained to me the family philosophy—"Since our family places great emphasis on education, [boy] fully accepts that the only guarantee for a good and stable future can be only achieved through outstanding education."

The third group is perhaps the most tragic: they are well-educated professionals who simply lack English-language skills. Often they come from the former Soviet Union, and in their home countries were engineers, medical professionals, and scientists. In the United States, they drive cabs and have to pretend to care about "Gothicism" in "A Rose for Emily" for the sake of another degree. For the most part, these clients actually send in their own papers and they get an edit from a native speaker. Sometimes they even pinch-hit for the brokers, doing papers on graduate-level physics and nursing themselves.

Term paper writing was never good money, but it was certainly fast money. For a freelancer, where any moment of slack time is unpaid time, term papers are just too tempting. Need $100 by Friday to keep the lights on? No sweat. Plenty of kids need ten pages on *Hamlet* by Thursday. Finals week is a gold mine. More than once the phone rang at midnight and the broker had an assignment. Six pages by 6:00 a.m.—the kid needs three hours to rewrite and hand in the paper by 9:00 or he won't graduate. "Cool," I'd say. "A hundred bucks a page." I'd get it, too, and when I didn't get it, I slept well anyway. Even DUMB CLIENTS could figure out that they'd be better off spending $600 on the model paper instead of $2,500 to repeat a course. Back in the days when a pulse and pay stub was sufficient to qualify for a mortgage, term papers—along with gigs for dot-com-era business magazines—helped me buy my first house.

Term paper work is also extremely easy, once you get the hang of it. It's like an old dance routine buried in one's muscle memory. You hear the tune—say, "Unlike the ancient Greek tragic playwrights, Shakespeare likes to insert humor in his tragedies"—and your body does the rest automatically. I'd just scan Google or databases like Questia.com for a few quotes from primary and secondary sources, create an argument based on whatever popped up from my search, write the introduction and underline the thesis statement, then fill in the empty spaces between quotes with whatever came to mind.

Getting the hang of it is tricky, though. Over the years, several of my friends wanted in on the term paper racket, and most of them couldn't handle it. They generally made the same fundamental error—they tried to write term papers. In the paper mill biz, the paper isn't important. The deadline, page count, and number of sources are. DUMB CLIENTS make up much of the trade. They have no idea whether or not Ophelia committed suicide or was secretly offed by Gertrude, but they know how to count to seven if they ordered seven pages.

I had a girlfriend who had been an attorney and a journalist, and she wanted to try a paper. I gave her a five-page job on leash laws in dog parks, and she came home that evening with over 50 pages of print outs, all articles and citations. She sat down to write. Three hours later she was rolling on the floor and crying. She had tried to write a paper instead of filling five pages. Another friend of mine spent hours trying to put together an eight-page paper on magical realism in Latin American fiction. At midnight she declared that it was impossible to write that many pages on books she had never read. She was still weeping, chain-smoking cigarettes, and shouting at me at 2:00 a.m. I took 20 minutes and finished the paper, mostly by extending sentences until all the paragraphs ended with an orphaned word on a line of its own.

The secret to the gig is to amuse yourself. I have to, really, as most paper topics are deadly boring. Once, I was asked to summarize in three pages the causes of the First World War (page one), the major battles and technological innovations of the war (page two), and to explain the aftermath of the war, including how it led to the Second World War (page three). Then there was this assignment for a composition class: six pages on why "apples [the fruit] are the best." You have to make your own fun. In business papers, I'd often cite Marxist sources. When given an open topic assignment on ethics, I'd write on the ethics of buying term papers, and even include the broker's website as a source. My own novels and short stories were the topic of many papers—several DUMB CLIENTS rate me as their favorite author and they've never even read me, or anyone else. Whenever papers needed to refer to a client's own life experiences, I'd give the student various sexual hang-ups.

It's not that I never felt a little skeevy writing papers. Mostly it was a game, and a way to subsidize my more interesting writing. Also, I've developed a few ideas of my own over the years. I don't have the academic credentials of composition experts, but I doubt many experts spent most of a decade writing between one and five term papers a day on virtually every subject. I know something they don't know; I know why students don't understand thesis statements, argumentative writing, or proper citations.

It's because students have never read term papers.

Imagine trying to write a novel, for a grade, under a tight deadline, without ever having read a novel. Instead, you meet once or twice a week with someone who is an expert in describing what novels are like. Novels are long stories, you see, that depict a "slice of life" featuring a middle-class protagonist. Psychological realism is prized in novels. Moral instruction was once fairly common in novels, but is now considered gauche. Novels end when the protagonist has an epiphany, such as "I am not happy. Also, neither is anybody else." Further, many long fictions are called novels even though they are really adventures, and these ersatz novels may take place in a fantastical setting and often depict wild criminal behaviors and simplified versions of international intrigues instead of middle-class quandaries. Sometimes there are pirates, but only so that a female character may swoon at their well-developed abdominal muscles. That's a novel. What are you waiting for? Start writing! *Underline your epiphany.*

There's another reason I never felt too badly about the job, though I am pleased to be done with papers. The students aren't only cheating themselves. They are being cheated by the schools that take tuition and give nothing in exchange. Last year, I was hired to write two one-page summaries of two short stories. Here are the client's instructions:

> i need you to write me two different story in all these listed under. The introduction of the story, the themes, topic and character, please not from internet, Or any posted web sites, because my professor will know if from internet this is the reason why i' m spending money on it.Not two much words, because i will still write it back in clsss go straight to the point and write me the conclusion at end of the two story, the second story different introduction, themes, topic and character. Thank you God Bless.

At the parties I go to, people start off laughing, but then they stop.

Acknowledgments

For a short book, Starve Better has a fair number of acknowledgments. First, there's Joi Brozek, who introduced me to the blogosophere, which in turn led me to write much of the material in this book. Tim Pratt and Heather Shaw published several of these pieces in their now sadly defunct fanzine *Flytrap*, as did Ron Kovach of *The Writer* magazine. Jessie Smith of *The Smart Set* helped me achieve my life's dream of being denounced as a whore in the national media. Thanks to Arachne Jericho for a real brainteaser of a question. Most of all, though, I should acknowledge all the people over the years who looked at my work and said to me, "You should put all these little essays together in a book; I'd buy a copy." I have forgotten most of your names, but of course you're sure to be reading this acknowledgement list now, so please write your name here: _____ .

NICK MAMATAS IS THE AUTHOR OF THREE AND A HALF novels, over seventy short stories, and hundreds of feature articles, and is also an editor and anthologist. His fiction has been nominated for the Bram Stoker and International Horror Guild awards and translated into German, Italian, and Greek; his editorial work with *Clarkesworld* earned the magazine World Fantasy and Hugo award nominations. Nick's reportage, short stories, and essays have appeared in venues such as *Razor*, *Asimov's Science Fiction*, *Silicon Alley Reporter*, the *Village Voice*, *The Smart Set*, *The Writer*, *Poets & Writers* and anthologies including Supernatural Noir and Lovecraft Unbound. He teaches at Western Connecticut State University in the MFA program in Creative and Professional Writing, was a visiting writer at Lake Forest College and the University of California, Riverside's Palm Desert Campus, and runs writing classes in the San Francisco Bay Area.